The Alchemist's Heir
Copyright© 2012 by John J. Mathis

Produced by CreateSpace, a DBA of On-Demand
Publishing, LLC

ISBN-13: 978-1469925431

ISBN-10: 1469925435

Contents

Author's Note

This is my first book. In the instance that this is my last book, I wanted to make sure I had something to say. This is why I have been writing and rewriting this over and over in my head for years and years. I have been blessed by many mentors along my path of self-discovery, and I wanted to share with you the fascination I had while discovering astral projection, reiki, Silva Mind Method, and other assorted rabbit holes I've explored. Each has contributed to who I am—and to who I am becoming. They have given me the tools to survive bankruptcy, a coma, nursing school, divorce, welfare, and several dogmas and "-isms." It is my hope that this book finds its way into the hands of those in need. It is my intention that something herein inspires you to get up one more time and to discover that within a crisis is a teacher and that you have the power to shape your reality.

Prologue

From the safety of his nightly slumber, the ancient wizard woke with a start. The scent of death was near. Bolting from the bed, he looked out the window to see the nature of the beast that had come for him. Fire was there to consume both him and his home. His tired nightshirt clung to his scarecrow frame for support as he ran to the other side of the house. Fire surrounded his home in its hateful embrace. Options and outcomes whirled through his mind as the wizard tried to think of any course of action that would save his life. Nothing came to mind. He was helpless.

He made his way slowly to the front porch, stepped briefly toward the maelstrom and sighed. He gradually embraced the swirling heat and arid smoke. If this was to be his end, then, like the mythical phoenix, he would surrender to it.

Suddenly, he saw the frantic movements of a shape near the edge of the woods. Someone was trying to put out this inferno with only a bucket of water! With stinging eyes, the wizard stood blinking in amazement. The person standing on the edge of the fire was not harmed by it. This person had no water supply, yet every time the person threw the bucket, water would shower forth as though the bucket were perpetually full.

The wizard stumbled forward a few steps to get a better look at his would-be rescuer. He was small. Two thoughts collided in his head. His hero was no more than a boy, and that the boy looked exactly as he did when he had been young so long ago. Stunned, the wizard watched his younger self heave bucket after bucket of water into the inferno. As the wizard opened his mouth to speak, a bomb exploded to his left. The heat had caused a tree to explode.

Still, his hero strove to put out the fire. When the wizard gazed at the boy, he was surprised to see his face had changed. It was no longer his younger self. This boy was a little chubby and a bit taller than before. The look of determination was the same though. For a moment, the boy stopped and looked squarely at the wizard. Shock thundered through the wizard's head as he realized the boy's identity.

The wizard closed his eyes as reality shifted. He opened his eyes again to see sunlight seeping in through the window of his bedroom. The radio alarm clock was playing a familiar country tune about those who truly live not standing outside the fire. The wizard walked to the bathroom, turned on the shower, and took off the T-shirt he wore as a nightshirt. While brushing his teeth, he thought he should call to see how the young man was feeling. Should he call this desire a compulsion or a burning desire? He snorted in amusement at the pun. Wiping toothpaste off his chin, he carried on with his morning rituals. To him, it was clear; he and his very own grandson would be facing a challenge side by side.

Chapter 1 – The Party

In the hazy summer afternoon, Tom sat on the front porch with a magnifying glass melting small holes into a dust-covered plastic model car. This was what happened to almost every model car he built. He would hastily put it together in a rush of excitement. Then, when the job was complete, he became disinterested. For weeks it would sit—unused and unappreciated. Eventually another model would appear, and the older one went to the Swiss cheese factory in the sky.

Little beads of sweat appeared on his neck and forearms under the high summer sun. Tom didn't notice though. He sat there with the magnifying glass in his hands and focused on melting a misshapen sunroof into the model car. It was some sort of race car ... a funny car, according to the box it came in. It was definitely funny-looking now! He snorted out loud, not at the joke, but at how lame it was.

It was the first week of summer vacation for Tom, and he was glad to have it. His freshman year at high school had not been fun at all. His older brother, Mark, had been a senior last year and was pretty much Tom's exact opposite. Mark was an academic all-star and a football all-star, and he worked part-time at a music store in the mall. Tom called himself an "all-scar." He was almost a foot shorter than his brother, his dark brown hair was a mess no matter how many times he combed it, and his chubby cheeks and tummy inspired his bother to start calling him Waddle. Once in the school cafeteria, his brother's friends were mocking him, and Tom told them all to go to hell. Unfortunately, his maturing voice cracked and an untimely, humiliating

1

falsetto came out of his mouth. Yeah, it was good to be out of school and away from the remarks of Mark and his moronic friends.

"Damn it!" shouted Tom.

While he had been daydreaming about the school year, his hand moved a bit and so had the magnifying glass. A bright red mark was now on the inside of his ankle.

"What I don't need is a hole in my ankle," said Tom.

He stood up, stepped on the car model to crush it, and then tossed the pieces in the bushes along the side of the porch. Tom walked into his house, morosely stomped up the stairs, and in his room shut himself off from the world. He lay in bed and stared at the ceiling. This summer was looking to be a pretty boring one. He had only two real friends, and they were either going on vacation to summer camp or lived too far away to get to his home.

Tom lived in an old farmhouse that his parents had been renovating as he grew up. It was deep in the country; the closest living souls to his house were a herd of cows in the field across a lonely gravel road. With both his parents working and his brother off in his own world of jerks, he settled into the fact that he would pretty much have the house to himself. With video games, the Internet, and his bicycle, he figured that it wouldn't be too bad. As he considered what kind of model car to buy the next time he went to the store, he drifted off to sleep.

Contrary to Tom's bedroom, the rest of the house was a flurry of activity. Mark had just graduated from high school, and the party for his graduation was tomorrow. Mark had spent most of the morning creating a banner that said, "Congratulations Mark!" He then took it out to the large oak tree that dominated the front of the house and strung up the sign in the low-lying branches. He stood with his hands on his hips and surveyed his handiwork.

"Looks pretty good, if I do say so myself!" said Mark to himself.

Mark picked up his T-shirt from the grass where he had discarded it to hang up the sign and tucked it into the back of his shorts. Mark liked to walk around without wearing his shirt. He was taking the rope back to the shed when he met his father.

Ray Miller was a handsome man. He looked more like Mark's older brother even though he was twenty-one years older. The only obvious difference was the way Ray's hands looked—callused and wise. They were both about 6 feet tall and had similar physiques. Mark's came from three years of playing football and working out with weights. Ray's came from working outside in the elements most of his life and from being a fireman for close to twenty years. Ray's energetic and no-nonsense attitude was second only to his work ethic. When something difficult needed to be done, he was the first to get started.

"Mark, come help me with this tent," said Ray.

"Why isn't Tom out here helping you?" asked Mark.

"Because he's inside helping your mother," said Ray.

"No, he isn't," said Mark. "He was sitting on the front porch when I last saw him."

Ray said, "Stop worrying what your brother is doing and help me."

Mark sighed; he knew that any further discussion with his father would end up getting him in trouble. Mark grabbed the end of the large tent and pulled it out with his father pulling on the other side. Once they positioned the tent by the back porch, Mark trotted back to the shed to get a hammer and the spikes to hold the tent poles in place. As he came back, he ran around the other side of the house to see if his brother was still sitting there like a statue. He did not find Tom, but he did find the broken, melted model. He brought it to his father.

"Dad, look at this."

Ray finished hammering a stake into the ground with a tent pole and then looked.

"What was that?" asked Ray.

"It's a model car that Tom destroyed. Why does he do stuff like that?" asked Mark.

"I don't know, Mark," said Ray in a slightly exasperated tone.

"He is his own person, and you are your own person. He just does things differently than you do."

With a rehearsed smirk, Mark said, "He does things differently compared with everyone I know. He's just plain weird."

"Well," said Ray, "when you go to the junior college next year, you'll meet lots of different people. You'll discover what weird really is."

Junior college was a sore spot for Mark. He wanted to go immediately to a four-year college, somewhere far away where he could really have some fun. However, money was tight at home, and the family had decided that Mark would go to community college for his first year so he could live at home while completing the basic college classes taught in the freshman year.

They resumed putting the tent up. It was a perfect size for covering the picnic table from the summer sun. Mark and his father had raised the tent and were tightening the ropes supporting the poles when Mrs. Miller came out with a glass of freshly made lemonade for each of them. Karen Miller was the perfect complement to her husband. Ray's favorite place was either walking through the woods or sitting by a campfire. Karen's favorite place was in the kitchen. When she wasn't working at the local Farmer's Bank as the manager, she was in the kitchen trying out recipes she had read in a magazine or seen on TV. Although she was not athletic or one to spend her free time outdoors, she always seemed to have a glow about her.

"You gentlemen look like you need something cold to drink," said Karen.

Both of them gladly took a break. The heat of the day was punishing, and the occasional breeze offered no reprieve. Ray sipped his drink, pausing occasionally to rub the side of the glass across his forehead. Mark quickly chugged the lemonade and then started chewing the rapidly melting ice. As they stood there chatting and drinking, talk turned to how each was progressing on the party preparations.

"Well," started Mark, "I got the stereo up from the basement last night and set it up in the living room. I created a couple of different

5

playlists on my mp3 player so we'll have different kinds of music during the party. I also grabbed the chairs that were down there, but I left them in the garage because they need to be cleaned up a bit."

Karen said, "That's great, sweetie. I have the potato salad, the deviled eggs, and five gallons of lemonade made. Once the sun goes down and it cools a bit, I will make some brownies and some peanut butter fudge."

"Yum!" said Mark enthusiastically.

"I got a case of hamburgers and hot dogs out of the freezer about half an hour ago," said Ray, "so they should be thawed out by tomorrow afternoon. Later I'll get some tomatoes, onions, and corn from the garden."

"So we still need to get to the store and pick up bread, pickles, lettuce and condiment stuff, right?" asked Mark. If there were any reason to take the car somewhere, Mark was always ready to go.

"Yes, but first, finish helping your father with the tent. When that's done, bring me a few tomatoes from the garden for dinner tonight. Then you can go to the store and pick up those things. While you're there, if you want, grab some balloons and streamers so that we can decorate the mailbox and the house."

"OK, Mom" said Mark with a radiant grin.

About twenty minutes later, Mark was leaving a light trail of dust hanging in the air as he sped down the gravel road heading for the grocery store. While he was gone, Karen seized the opportunity to talk to Ray. She had been observing Tom for a few weeks now and watched as he became more withdrawn and sullen. She had an idea brewing that she wanted to run past Ray without either of the boys around. She found Ray wiping down the wooden picnic table he had pulled from under a pair of silver maple trees that shaded the back of their home.

"Ray, why are you pulling the table out from the shade of the trees?"

"The cows and silver maples are saying it's going to rain pretty soon. I think we should keep people close to the house if that's the case."

Ray learned from his dad a long time ago that when there is a breeze and the silver maple trees turn their leaves over so that the silvery bottom is showing, rain would not be too far away. The cows had also congregated into one corner of the pasture as well, which supported his suspicions. Ray had a wonderful respect for nature and learned at a young age from his father to listen to Nature when she spoke to you. Sometimes she whispered; sometimes she roared.

"We need to talk," said Karen as she sat down on the edge of the table Ray had just cleaned.

Ray liked to call a discussion either a sit-down talk or a stand-up talk. Sensing that this would be a sit-down talk, he grabbed his watery lemonade, tucked his cleaning rag into the top of his overalls, and sat down. He sipped from his glass and waited.

"Tom has not been his usual self the past couple of weeks. He's become more distant and spends a lot of time in his room."

"Has he helped you at all today?" asked Ray.

"No, and that is one of my points. He usually volunteers to help out around the house, but recently he will only do the things that I repeatedly ask him to do. I deliberately made a bunch of noise in the kitchen to see if he would come down and help. He didn't."

Ray nodded quietly in agreement. Most teenaged boys have selective hearing unless food or money was involved. However, he had seen some changes too, but had said nothing up to now. Karen continued.

"I know he had it rough this year in school, but he really needs to find a way to step outside the shadow ... and the influence of his brother. He needs to find out who he is and not what others think he should be. I want him to be positive—positive about himself, his friends, and his life," said Karen. Her words came out so fast that it surprised her a bit. After a moment of quiet thought, she continued.

"I see him as being indifferent right now. I want him to start thinking positive thoughts before he starts to self-destruct."

Without a word, Ray stood up and walked over to where the tools from raising the tent still lay. He picked up a multicolored chunk of melted and jagged plastic. He sat it in front of his wife.

"This is what he did this morning when I thought he was inside helping you," stated Ray.

She picked up the broken and grossly distorted remnants of the model and turned it over and over in her hands. As she did so, her eyes filled with tears, which glided silently down her worried face.

Mentally, Ray told himself that this was going to be a long sit-down talk and the party preparations could wait. He moved next to his wife and put an arm around her. While Tom napped in his room, his parents started making plans to help him. What no one realized at the time was that it was going to change his life dramatically forever.

About dinnertime, the smells from the kitchen beckoned Tom from his sleep. He meandered down the stairs and sat at the kitchen table. His mom looked up from the pan of fried chicken and saw him looking vacantly at her. The matted hair on his head told Karen that he had slept the better part of the day away. This fact hardened her resolve with respect to the decision she and Ray had come to earlier.

She walked over to the cabinet, pulled out four plates, and sat them in front of him. Tom took the not so subtle hint and began to set the table for dinner. Soon the table disappeared from view as plates of fried chicken, mashed potatoes with parsley, green beans with bacon, and a robust bowl of salad appeared. As if on cue, both Ray and Mark appeared, coming from opposite sides of the house. Everyone took their seats and a brief silence descended on the table.

"Great Creator," intoned Ray, "we thank you for this bounty. May we use it to strengthen our hearts, bodies, minds, and spirits. Protect us as we continue to grow and mature until we again return to you."

"Amen," echoed in the room. Soon the clanking of silverware on plates was the only sound to be heard. Gradually, a discussion started about the party tomorrow. Topics concerning the weather, who would be coming to the party, what kind of gifts might be given, and the like were passed around like plates of food.

While this discussion went on around him, Tom stared vacantly into his plate. He secretly wished that this party would hurry up and be over with because it meant an entire day devoted to how wonderful his brother was. He felt that pretty much every day was that type of day. Soon he was aware that he had eaten everything on his plate except for the green beans. He hated green beans, but he loved the bits of bacon mixed in with them. So, he sat and delicately fished out the small chunks of bacon and then asked to be excused.

"No, you can finish the green beans first, and then you can clean up the kitchen for your mother," said Ray.

"Why?" whined Tom.

"Because you wasted the entire day today lying around," said Ray.

"Why do I have to do anything for this stupid party anyway? It all about Mark ... it's always all about Mark!" complained Tom.

"Yeah, it's all about me," said Mark in a mocking tone. "It's not my fault you sit on your butt all day with your video games or surfing the Internet. If you don't want to have a life, then fine, but don't have a hissy fit because I have one."

"Why don't you go off somewhere and compliment yourself," said Tom snidely.

"Enough!" said Ray in a threatening tone.

"May I be excused, please? I need to go compliment myself,"

said Mark sarcastically.

"Yes, Mark. We need to talk with your brother," said Karen before things escalated.

"OK, Mom," said Mark with an air of satisfaction. After he got up, he locked eyes with his brother, flexed his pectoralis muscles, and walked upstairs.

Tom stared back at him and just repeated the word *jerk* over and over in his head. He wasn't dumb enough to give Mark the satisfaction of getting himself into more trouble.

Once Mark cleared the room, Ray scooted his chair closer to Tom. Karen began moving dishes to the sink and putting away the leftover food. Ray spoke first.

"Tom, this temper tantrum is extremely out of character for you and apparently has been building for quite some time. Several times this past year your brother and you have locked horns on a couple of issues. Most of that is just normal growing up. But the two of you are very different. I know that Mark has a different set of priorities than you have. Those differences are not a bad thing, nor should they be made out to be.

I also know that he and his friends have the tendency to say mean and derogatory things to you. Although this is not nice, nor is it right, it is a burden that younger siblings have to deal with on a regular basis. The bright side is that you will not have to bear so much since he will no longer be in school with you. You won't have to be so defensive.

"You are still trying to find out who you are and what you stand for at this age. It is harder for you to make those kinds of decisions when you have your brother, his friends, television, movies, music, and your peers all telling you to be a certain way. The only way for you to know who you really are is to get as many of those distractions away from you as possible … at least for a while."

At this point, Tom was scared. He had no idea where his dad was going with this idea. Was he going to lose TV privileges for a couple of weeks? Was he going to lose the Internet? If he couldn't check his Facebook page for two weeks, he would go crazy! Maybe his brother was going to move away? Maybe they were going to send one of them to camp? As he wondered all these things, his mother sat down and gazed kindly across the table at him.

"Tommy," said Karen, "I talked to your dad this afternoon about how unhappy you appear to be. I know that you feel that you don't measure up to your brother. I know that you resent him for his successes. I also know that he can be full of himself at times and you don't appreciate it. But, instead of trying to come out from his shadow, you seem to hide deeper within it and then complain that you can't see. We want to help you from hiding. Do you understand?"

Silence filled the space. Tom ventured a glance toward his mom and saw that she was expecting an answer. Tom chose his words cautiously but sincerely.

"I am just tired of no one paying attention to me. It ticks me off," said Tom.

"If you want to have people pay attention to you, you need to do something worthy of attention. Hiding in your bedroom won't get you anywhere," said Ray.

"This is not the way to go about it," said Karen. As she said that, she pulled the dish towel off the table and revealed the lumpy burned mess of a model car.

Tom began to cry. "I don't know what to do."

Karen pulled her chair around to Tom. She sat down and put her arm around him. She hugged him and stroked his hair. Remembering the axiom about a spoonful of sugar, she gently lifted his quivering chin and gave him a conspiratorial grin.

"Tommy, we're going to help you to know what to do. We are going to share something with you that we have not shared with Mark. It's something very special."

Immediately, Tom stopped crying. It was not so much that they were going to give him something that they had not given Mark as it was the tone of his mother's voice. It was as if she were whispering what she was going to give him for Christmas. Although a bit confused, he gave her his full attention.

Karen continued. "We are going to help you to see the world from a very different perspective. You are going to learn how to think in completely different ways. You will learn new ways to use your mind, to shape the course of your life, and how to ask the Universe to attend to your every wish."

"Are you going to teach me to be a wizard or something?" asked Tom incredulously.

"No, I am not going to teach you anything," said Karen. "But we have made arrangements with someone who will. Someone who you might call a wizard."

"Who is it?" asked Tom excitedly.

"We're not going to tell you right now. But I will tell you this: You will see him here tomorrow," said Ray.

"There's a wizard coming to Mark's graduation party tomorrow? Who do we know who is a wizard? Is there really such a thing as a wizard?" Tom was full of questions.

"We're not going to tell you everything tonight. You need to get your chores done and then get to bed. Tomorrow will be a long day ...even longer for you," said Ray. Karen nodded in agreement as a sly grin slowly spread across her face.

Tom protested a few more times, but his parents were not going to give up any more information. He finally did the chores as he was told but was almost completely unaware that he was doing something he despised. His head was full of thoughts and wondering what the day would hold for him tomorrow. As he went to sleep that night, he did not even think of Mark. Instead, he drifted off to sleep and dreamed of his school science lab surrounded by mirrors. In the lab, a benevolent wizard from one of his video games was waiting there for him. He escorted Tom to each mirror and asked him to look into it. In each mirror, he saw a different part of his ideal self. In one, he was an honor roll student. In another, he was the school's new quarterback. In yet another mirror, he saw himself with a raven-haired girlfriend. Any of these futures were available to him. He only needed to choose. As he slept, he smiled.

Down the hall, Karen and Ray were taking turns talking on the telephone to Tom's "wizard". He chuckled at the inference and said he preferred to be known as an alchemist. They wanted to make sure that he was aware of what was going on with Tom. With the best of intentions, they started to make plans for the alchemist's heir and his eventual arrival.

The next day was quite different from the day before, in many ways. It had rained that night and much cooler temperatures had moved in for the day of Mark's party. The day was also quite different because Tom was the first person up. He was all smiles; he helped his mom in the kitchen with setting out dishes and plates of food, offered to get his dad more chairs when they were needed ... he was even polite to his brother. It was as if Santa Claus were coming to visit in person.

Slowly, friends and family began to trickle into the house. As Tom wandered around the party trying to decide which one was the "wizard," no one in particular stood out. It couldn't be his Uncle Randy, who went around asking people to pull his finger. It couldn't be Mr. Tibbs from the tractor dealership. He pretty much took root in front of the deviled eggs all afternoon. It obviously couldn't be Ms. Shawna ... she seemed to be readjusting her underwear whenever she thought no one was looking. As the day drew on, ordinary people came and went. Tom's assessment was always the same. Each time someone new showed up, Tom would be the first to greet him or her. He hoped that there would be a glimmer in the person's eye ... some tell-tale sign that someone was a "wizard." Yet, no one like that appeared.

As the sun began its daily surrender, a gnawing doubt began to grow in Tom's mind. It finally took shape: His parents were just feeding him a line of bull. They just wanted him to play nice while the party took place. At first he didn't want to believe that they would do something like that to him. However, the more he stewed about it, the more sense it made. They did not want him ruining Mark's party. Of course they were looking out for Mark. Mark has always been the favorite one. Behind his eyes, anyone could see the thunderstorm brewing.

The longer he thought about this fact, the angrier he became. He felt truly betrayed, being set up by his own parents. His anger had become so great that he no longer wanted to talk to or be seen by anyone. So, he headed straight for his bedroom. He bounded up to the top of the stairs two at a time. He stormed into his room, slammed the door, and flipped on the light. Materializing in the corner of his room was an old man.

"Jesus!" shouted Tom. The appearance of someone in his room startled him so badly that it took a second for him to realize that it was his grandfather.

"Hello there, Thomas," said William with a lopsided grin. "I appreciate the comparison but ... it's just Grandpa."

William was Ray's father. This father and son were more physical opposites than Ray and Mark. William was in his early seventies but looked to be more about fifty years old. He had hair that was not white and was not silver but something in between. He wore a close-cut goatee and glasses, which he frequently looked over the top of when he talked to people. He was about six feet tall and a bit pudgy around the middle. His gray wool jacket was draped across his knee, and the black T-shirt that he wore still revealed the arms of someone who had worked as a carpenter most of his life. These days, he was the owner of a cabinet manufacturing company. As he tells the story, he didn't swing a hammer much any more, but he just couldn't stay away from the smell of freshly cut wood.

"Grandpa, what are you doing here?" asked Tom.

"Isn't it obvious? I am here for Mark's graduation party. Why are you here?"

"Uh, Grandpa, I live here."

"Hmm. I thought I heard that you were unhappy living here."

"Oh, did you talk to Mom and Dad?" asked Tom as his defenses began to rise.

"I didn't have to. I saw it in your eyes when I got here today."

Tom did not know what to say. He stared at the floor for a second or two as his grandfather continued.

"So, are you going to get packed or what?"

"What do you mean?" asked Tom.

"What I mean is that I am supposed to take you to the wizard, boy. Are you going to stand around with your jaw dragging the ground or are you going to get a move on and come with me?"

Tom exploded into action. He grabbed a duffel bag and began

stuffing in clothes at random, all the while asking questions.

"Where are we going? Do you know who the wizard is? How far away is it?"

Grandpa William just smiled the knowing smile of a person who knows a secret and is on the verge of telling. Finally, Tom was finished packing—not because he knew he had all the things that he needed, but because the bag was full.

"OK, Thomas, grab your jacket and your bag," said William.

"What about Mom and Dad? I need to tell them goodbye."

"Nope, we have to leave now if I am going to get you to where we need to be on time," said William.

"But I need to get my allowance from Dad."

"Nope, we have to leave right this minute or the whole thing is off," said William.

Still dizzy from the sudden change of events, Tom stumbled after his grandfather, who led him out to the driveway. Tom tossed his belongings into the back of his grandfather's Jeep and got in the passenger seat. As William got to the Jeep, he turned and looked back at the front porch of the house. He saw both Ray and Karen standing there. It was as if they were in a separate bubble in time and space as they stood in quiet concern and hopefulness. Meanwhile the party lights swung in the breeze and danced to the music Mark had selected yesterday. William saw each reality and acknowledged both of them. He blew them a kiss, hopped into the Jeep, and drove off into the evening twilight.

Once on the highway, the road noise was a bit distracting and Tom realized that there would not be any way they could have a detailed discussion. William could see that Tom was full of questions and anticipation. He had to smile to himself—he too felt the same way. They each had their thoughts of anticipation to keep them occupied as they sped down the moonlit highway. After a while, the excitement wore off for Tom and the steady hum of the Jeep's tires on the highway was hypnotic. Slowly, he started to drift off to sleep. His grandfather saw this and asked Tom if he was still awake.

"Hmm...?" said a groggy Tom.

"Repeat what I say. Every day and in every way..." said William.

"Every day and in every way..." mumbled Tom.

"I am getting better and better," intoned William.

"I am getting better and better," whispered Tom.

Grandfather and grandson repeated this line over and over seven times before Tom started snoring. William smiled. As he continued driving through the night, he softly hummed the tune about being off to see a wizard.

Chapter 2 – Grandpa

The first thing Tom noticed the next morning was that it was way too bright in his room. He always kept the curtains closed so that he could sleep in as late as possible. He finally opened his eyes to see that he was not in his room at all. Finally, the sequence of events flooded back to him—the rapid departure, the long drive, and some sort of chant before waking up here. What a place "here" was!

Tom did not really know much about his grandpa except that he was a really good carpenter who taught others to be just as good. Eventually, he had a few people who wanted to work only for him, so he started a company. The company did really well, because the stuff they made was beautiful and unique. People from all over the world ordered his work off the Internet. There was no one to share this success with, as his grandma had divorced William before Tom was born and Grandpa had never remarried. There was also a falling out between William and Ray before either Mark or Tom were even born, but, as Ray would put it, there had been some fence mending along the way.

From what Tom knew, Grandpa was also a bit of a nut. He grew a lot of different herbs and plants, which he used in his food, made into teas or just hung around the house. He also built most of his own furniture. Ray called it Mission Style, but Tom never really understood what that meant until now. He looked up from the couch he had been sleeping on, rubbed the sleep from his eyes, and truly looked around the place. Dominating the room was a thirty-foot-tall fireplace made from river stone. There were stones about the size of a tennis ball to as big as a football. They were of varying colors, but all of them were very smooth and polished looking. Some wrought-iron tools and a set of bellows flanked the fireplace. Tom had never seen bellows before. He thought it looked like a cross between an accordion and bagpipes. The ceiling reminded him of a church, as you could see right up to the roof and the wooden beams that supported it were in the room itself. He noticed that there were small lights and speakers mounted up there. Tom smiled to himself. Grandpa went and built himself a nightclub.

The great room had wooden end tables and wrought-iron floor lamps. The coffee table in the middle of the room had a wooden base, but the top of it was a solid piece of stone with different types of sparkling crystals in it. Grandpa had polished it so it looked like the river stones and then covered it with some sort of protective sealant. It seemed so inviting that Tom reached out to touch it. He was surprised to feel that it was warm to touch. The wooden floors were very dark and smooth, but they did not have the luster that the rest of the wood had.

He sat up on the couch, slowly swung his legs out from the blanket and stared around the room some more. There were paneled doors on either side of the fireplace. Tom assumed that they led to bedrooms. He did not know which one was his grandpa's so he did not try to venture into them. Along the right-hand side of the great room was a hallway. He got up, yawned, and shuffled down the hall as he scratched his riotous mop of hair. He saw all sorts of weird stuff. Grandpa had Asian pictures on the wall of some lady riding a dragon.

He also had pictures of a bunch of bald-headed people wearing gold and red colored robes. They were a band of some sort because they had bells and other instruments in front of them. He also noticed that they had really big bowls in front of them too. For as little as these guys looked, they apparently ate a whole lot.

On the opposite wall, Grandpa had hung up pictures and art from some American Indians. The first thing he thought was that the Indians looked a lot like the Asian dudes from the other wall. They had longer hair and the clothing was different, but there was still something about them that made Tom think that they were really the same people. Grandpa had hung some small pottery pieces and some jewelry on the wall as well. One of the pieces looked like a dude jamming on the tenor sax.

"That's Kokopelli," said Grandpa.

"Koko - who?" asked Tom. He had not heard William come up behind him.

"Kokopelli ... a favorite of mine and of the Anasazi people. He was one of their gods who represented success in growing crops, catching food, and making babies."

"Why is he playing the tenor sax?" asked Tom.

"Well, he was probably playing a wooden flute since this was going on well before the time Jesus was born. He probably used it to announce his arrival, to call in a good rain shower, or maybe to seduce young virgins," said William with a wink.

"Grandpa!" said Tom in a shocked tone.

"Come on, Thomas," said William with a growing smile, "I may be old, but I am not daft. Now come with me because I want to give you the grand tour."

William took his grandson around the house and property. As it turned out this originally had been his secret fishing spot, and over the decades he had added more and more to it. Most of the place was constructed from reclaimed timber from the local area barns and an old railroad trestle up river that had been replaced by a metal one.

Over the years the cabin grew into a house. Then the house grew into a lodge with extra rooms and baths. Under the house was a basement that hid the garage, an office, an exercise room, and a library. It held one of the largest collections of books that Tom had ever seen outside of a public library. There were sixty bookcases that stood taller than his grandfather was, and almost all of them were completely full.

"Grandpa, you have an entire bookstore in your basement!" exclaimed Tom.

"Well, it is a lot of books, but they are like old friends to me. Once I get to know them, I just can't bear to part with them. So I build them a home, and then I come here and visit them once in a while."

"Grandpa, you could get the all the books you will ever need right on the Internet. Why are you holding on to all of these?"

"Because, Thomas, you cannot cozy up to the fireplace with a drink on a chilly night with a computer. You cannot take the computer to bed with you and not worry about it falling as you go to sleep. You cannot lounge in a bathtub with a computer. You cannot feel the warm texture of the page under your fingers with a computer. For me, reading is a visceral experience."

"What about audio books or the e-readers they have out there?"

"Thomas, although I appreciate technology, I refuse to be owned by it."

"OK," he giggled. "I guess you're right. Still, it's a lot of books."

"Thomas, never be shy about spending money when it comes to education or travel. The things you learn can never be taken away from you."

As they were heading to the back of the basement, it suddenly dawned on Tom that they had not seen a television. He burst out, "Grandpa, you don't have a TV!"

"In the past few years it has just become a tool for rotting people's brains out. People don't think for themselves anymore because the news tells them what to think, the commercials tell them what to buy, and the shows tell them how to act. The person who said 'Kill your TV' was a genius."

Tom was about to protest when he saw his grandpa open a door, walk into complete nothingness, and disappear.

"Grandpa!" Tom shouted.

"Oops! Sorry about that, I don't usually use the light."

William came back and turned on a light switch that was a few feet inside the doorway. A tunnel had been dug into the layers of stone in a gentle downward angle with a slight curve to the right. It looked like a secret passageway that would have existed in a castle.

"Now, this may be a little scary," said William, "but I think it's pretty neat. A few years ago I had a heat pump installed in the basement so that the natural thermal dynamics of the ground would cool the place in the summer and warm it in the winter. As luck would have it, we discovered a natural spring. So now I have heating, cooling, and all the fresh water I can ever use."

They continued walking until they got to the heat pump. It was kind of loud with a humming and a whirring sound mixed up into one noise.

"Grandpa, it sounds like your tires on the highway when we drove here."

"Hmm. So it does," said William with a knowing smile.

"Where's the rest of the tunnel go to?" asked Tom.

"It goes to the barn behind the house. That's where I keep all my toys."

"Why did you build a tunnel from here to your barn?"

William paused for a second and then responded with his trademark lopsided smile, "Because I thought it would be cool."

Tom smiled back and followed his grandpa to the next discovery.

After another hundred feet or so they came to another door. Through this door and up a stairway to another door was another office. This one in particular was much different than the one he saw in the house. This one had blueprints for different kinds of armoires, closets, bookcases, and odd-looking chests of drawers with wide bottoms. There were several file cabinets covered with little notes, magnets, and pictures. Tom recognized pictures of his family. Some he did not recognize.

"Who's this?" asked Tom.

"That ... is a picture of your grandmother."

Tom stared long at the picture; he had never seen a picture of her looking so young. She was pretty looking in an old photograph sort of way. She had a wide smile and a crinkle above her nose as though she had heard something really funny. His recognized that crinkle because both Mark and their dad had the same crinkle when they laughed really hard.

"Why did she leave?" asked Tom.

"Only she really knows for sure," said William.

"Do you still love her?"

William thought for a second before responding, "I still love the thought of her."

"Did you try to talk to her before she died?"

"Tom, anything we would have wanted to say to each other here will have to wait until we're both over there," said William.

Tom felt bad for asking all of those questions and said so. William nodded his head in understanding. Her eyes and smile inspired a degree of familiarity he had never known. Suddenly, he felt as if he needed to know her; however, it would have to wait for now.

"Come on, Tom," said William. "There's more to see."

"What was her name, Grandpa?"

"Ruth. Her name was Ruth," said William as he ventured deeper into the barn.

Calling this place a barn was a real misnomer, because there was neither an animal nor any hay in sight. This looked more like a mad scientist's lab with all sorts of odd and strange looking equipment. One machine looked like a display of metallic lollipops. William saw him looking at this machine, so he walked over to it and turned it on. A small hum filled the room.

"Watch this," said William excitedly.

As he flipped a switch, a small blue spark jumped from one of the lollipops to another. Then it jumped from the second to another. There were five rows of five and the bolt jumped from one to the other until it finished the row. Then it jumped to the row directly below it and traced its way back. Once it got to the bottom of the row, it went to the last lollipop and disappeared.

William touched a couple of unseen controls, and the blue bolt got larger and moved quicker through the maze. Soon, it started jumping out of order with electricity dancing left and right, making dangerous crackling noises. Suddenly, they synchronized, and the whole display illuminated with a deep blue glow. A loud snap cracked the air, and a bluish white bolt of electricity shot straight up and hit a metal plate mounted about ten feet above them. With a smile, William turned off the machine and walked over to a light switch. He flipped the switch, and a light bulb a few feet away from the plate briefly lit and then dimmed into darkness.

"What the heck was that?" shouted Tom.

"That was me sending electricity through the air and lighting a light bulb."

"That was absolutely the coolest thing I have ever seen! My grandpa can throw lightning!"

"Thank you," said William. "I guess you can call me Zeus ... or Tesla."

"Huh?" said Tom.

"Never mind, Thomas. It reminds me, though, that we need to start on your education over breakfast."

"What do you mean, Grandpa?"

"What it means is that we need to get down to business now that you have seen the place. What you have not yet figured out, my boy, is that you are now in wizard training."

Tom sputtered. "What!? *You* are the wizard that everyone told me about?"

With a twinkle in his eye and a wry smile on his face, William leaned in a bit closer to Tom and almost whispered in order to capture his attention. He said, "What do *you* think? I have a castle in the woods. I have my magic library of spells and potions. I have a disguised laboratory. I have secret passages, and I can throw lightning. How much more proof do you need?"

28

"Do something really magical, like float or disappear."

"OK, how about this. You think about something that happened in your life and I will guess it."

Tom agreed. He thought about the stupid nickname that his brother had for him. "Waddle" was not a name that he or his brother used at home. That torture was exclusive to school. As he stood there looking at the ground and thinking about the stupid name, his grandpa hummed a low-pitched note.

He looked up to see his grandfather standing there with his eyes closed. He was breathing deeply and slowly. He stood there almost a minute before he spoke.

"I am seeing an order form for a client I recently spoke to. His name is Davis Waddell. I am also seeing a family of ducks crossing a road. Ducks waddle when they walk, so I am guessing that you want me to say the word 'waddle.'"

"Holy crap," said Tom softly.

"Indeed," William smiled. "Come on, let's waddle up to the house and have some breakfast."

Tom followed his grandfather quietly as he tried to wrap his brain around what had just happened. There was no way he could have pulled that out of the thin air. But he did! His grandfather had just stood there and in all of the words in the world, he had said the one word that Tom was holding in his mind. He stumbled as he walked back to the house and wondered where Grandpa could have possibly learned to do such a thing.

"Grandpa, are you a wizard ... like, for real?"

With an enigmatic smile, William replied, "No ... and yes."

Chapter 3 – Grandpa's Friends

Tom was pleased to find out that Grandpa was a pretty decent cook too. He sat in silence, watching his grandpa with a newfound respect. Grandpa had come to family gatherings and a couple of Mark's football games; he'd popped in unannounced occasionally. But out of all of these occasions, Tom could never remember him having the air about him of a psychic or wizard or anything in particular. He had been just ... Grandpa.

He looked up at his grandpa as he walked in from a large sunlit patio with a handful of various herbs. He diced them up very fine and added them to the bowl of scrambled eggs. He remained intent on making breakfast, however, he casually glanced sidelong at Tom now and then to see how his grandson was processing all of the new information being given to him. When he noticed that was Tom watching him and not thinking about the morning thus far, he decided to give him more to think about.

"Tom, what kind of hobbies do you have other than watching TV and destroying model cars?"

"Well," said Tom, feeling a bit embarrassed, "I play video games and I surf the 'net."

"Surf?" asked William.

"Yeah, I go onto the Internet and I just go wherever I want."

"You follow your own curiosity and instincts then, right?"

"I guess so," said Tom.

"OK then! I want you to follow your curiosity and instincts about what we saw in the laboratory...I mean barn."

"Your barn is your laboratory? I guess that makes sense.

You do experiments in there. Do you want me to go out there and figure out how it works?"

"No, Tom. Not yet at least. What I am going to do is point you in different directions, but I want you to follow that path and then come back to me and tell me what you have found and what you think about your findings."

"Aw, man ... that sounds like a book report," whined Tom.

"Don't think of it as a book report, Tom. Think of it like this: We're two explorers in the woods of a land we have never been to before now. We are trying to learn as much as we can about this land. The best way to do this is to send scouting parties into the woods, learn and record everything we see, and then come back at nightfall to report our findings to each other so that we can each benefit from the other's experience."

"Grandpa, it's just the woods. I already know everything that's out there. Bugs, weeds, trees, and some critters. What's the point?"

William put down the wooden spoon he was using. He stared at Tom with an intensity that demanded his attention. It had the desired effect. William continued very deliberately.

"The point is that you already have the capacity to be what you call a wizard by having curiosity, imagination, and intuition. Once we have given you a good foundation from which to jump, we can dive into the far more interesting things ... like reading minds. Besides, when you think you know what to expect, you limit yourself from experiencing ... the unexpected."

William moved the skillet of cooking eggs off of the heat of the stove and walked to the patio again. This time he went outside the glass enclosure and whistled loudly. Tom got up and followed his grandpa to the patio. The room was a combination lounge and greenhouse with raised gardens surrounding a couch, a chair, and a table that held books and magazines. The barking of dogs grabbed his attention from the table, and he walked outside to join his grandpa. Two of the biggest dogs Tom had ever seen charged out of the woods and toward the house. They not so much ran as galloped toward them.

"Don't worry, Tom. They're big but they are just goofballs. Think of them as really large puppies."

The dogs came up the side of the hill that the house was nestled into and ran right past them. Their barks echoed as they circled the house. Soon they reappeared and ran a couple of excited laps around grandfather and grandson. Eventually they settled and came to sit in front of William and Tom.

Up close, they were huge. Sitting up on their hind legs, they almost looked Tom right in the eye. The two were very hairy. Around their eyes and mouth were patches of tan-colored fur, but aside from that, they were as black as night. They panted like sprinters after running a race. As they got more settled, William introduced them to Tom as if they were friends of his.

"Tom, this big fellow here is Siddhartha. Sid is a six-year-old Tibetan mastiff. He tends to be a bit more aloof than most dogs, so he will not always come when you call. He has other priorities. He is polite, just not terribly social."

"Uh-huh," said Tom, who was still getting used to their enormous size.

"Sid, this is my grandson, Tom. He will be staying with us

for a while."

Sid reached out his right paw as if to shake hands.

"Should I?" asked Tom.

"Sure. You don't want to insult him, do you?"

Not wanting to insult the massive canine, Tom reached out and gently took his enormous mud-speckled paw. Shaking it gingerly, he said, "Hi, Sid. Nice to meet you."

Sid made a short woof sound that seemed to originate deep within the earth and ricochet off the back of the house. With the essential greeting completed, Sid turned around and galloped off into the woods again, leaving his companion.

The sound of a thumping tail pummeling the ground brought their attention back to the other dog. The only visual difference between the two dogs appeared to be that Sid weighed about twenty pounds more than his partner. However, behavioral differences soon became apparent. This dog stood up and walked directly in front of Tom. It then sat down and put its head under Tom's hand. Instinctively, Tom began scratching the dog behind the ears.

"This is Quan Yin. As you can see, Quan is much friendlier than Sid. She loves everyone she meets. Sid will warm up to you over time...especially now that Quan has given her seal of approval."

As if to accentuate the fact, Quan rolled over onto her back and waited to be scratched. Tom smiled softly and scratched her chest and belly. Again, her tail thumped in approval.

"While you're doing that, I want you to tap her sternum," said William.

"What? Tap her sternly?"

"No," chuckled William. "I want you to tap her breastbone about where her heart would be."

Following his grandpa's instruction, he began tapping her sternum. He started softly but gradually tapped harder until Quan's tail started wagging again. Tom continued for a few minutes. He was about to ask how much longer he was supposed to do this when Quan got up, nuzzled his face with her wet nose, and then took off for the woods just as Sid had done.

"Well, it looks as though you have made a new friend your first day here."

Tom smiled. "Why did they take off into the woods like that? Why did you have me thump her in the chest?"

"Excellent questions. I think you should venture into the library and see if there are any books down there about them. We'll address immune response and T cells another day."

Tom issued a quick sigh. "Grandpa, the Internet will have all the information I need. Why can't I use that?"

"Tom, the Internet may have all the answers about everything, but I am only interested in you finding the answers to specific questions. Pretend that I have put restrictions on the Internet so that you can only go to the areas that I have permitted."

"Grandpa, it would be so much easier to use the computer though," whined Tom.

"Easier is not always better. Some men live lifetimes

without learning that."

Tom sighed. He followed his grandpa back to the breakfast they had started earlier. As they sat down to eat finally, William asked Tom a question.

"So, when you told me you knew what was in the woods, did you think about two big dogs out there?"

"No," said Tom.

"Hmm...," William replied vaguely. Again he could see the wheels turning. He smiled, and they both finished their breakfast in silence.

After breakfast was done and the dishes cleared from the table, William gave Tom a quick hug and some instructions.

"OK, I have to run into town and pick up a few things. While I am gone, have a go in the library and teach me some things about the mastiffs. If any other book on the shelves down there catches your eye, feel free to have a look. Just remember, your goal is to look up the dogs. After you have done that, you can indulge your curiosity."

"Can't I go with you?" asked Tom.

"Not on this trip. However, I don't see why you can't come with me on any other trip."

Tom pouted slightly, "OK, I guess."

Grabbing his denim jacket and keys from the beige marble countertop, he announced that he would be back in a couple of hours. Off he went. From the kitchen, Tom heard his grandpa start the Jeep and then saw it bump along the dirt trail, turn by a cluster of trees, and disappear from sight. Tom opened the silver-faced refrigerator and found some apple juice. He poured himself a glass and then headed down the steps to the library.

Grandpa's library was actually a decent place to hang out. It was cool and quiet, and it had a neat smell that Tom could not identify. It was a sweet smell, as if someone had burned leaves a few weeks ago. Although he usually did not like the smell of smoke, this did not seem bad at all. As he looked through all the books, he began to recognize their organization. They were grouped by subject matter, and then they were arranged alphabetically by title.

Some of the books were predictable, as they pertained to carpentry and plan design. He found another bookcase that had nothing but classic American writers. Some names he recognized: Steinbeck, Hemingway, Twain, Poe, and Orwell. Other names he did not recognize: Silva, Dyer, Bach, Gardner, Virtue, and Manly P. Hall. He continued to another bookcase.

This bookcase had a bunch of religious books. There were books on Buddhism, Confucianism, Catholicism, Christianity, Hindu, Judaism, Wicca, and Zoasterism. He had never seen so many "-isms" in one place before. How in the world could so many religions exist? He knew from history class that people always seemed to be fighting about one religion being better than another. On the shelf, they all looked about the same to him.

Tom wasn't finding the book he wanted. He went over to the set of overstuffed chairs in the middle of the room. A fireplace against the far wall faced the chairs. On the opposite sides of the fireplace were small windows that let sunlight into the room. It then occurred to Tom that they were underground. How could there be light or windows there? Tom walked over to one of the windows and pulled back the curtain only to be dazzled with sunlight. Once his eyes adjusted, he noticed that a small alcove was dug into the wall and a mirror had been placed inside of it. Looking up into the alcove he saw the glass roof of the patio. He thought it was pretty cool how Grandpa managed to get sunlight into the basement.

Tom walked back to the center of the room and sat down on one of the chairs. His gaze rested on the table in front of him. He was not too surprised to see a book on Tibetan mastiffs already sitting there.

"Now how did he know I'd need help finding this?" wondered Tom aloud.

He flipped on a light and started to read.

Chapter 4 – Geniuses and Wizards

The Tibetan mastiff is an ancient and rare breed of canines. In fact, it's thought to be one of the oldest breeds in existence today. Tibetan mastiffs may have been around as early as the Stone or Bronze Age. That's around 3000 BC! Some believe that they were used as guard dogs in ancient China from 1000 BC. It can be proven that the Tibetan mastiff has remained unchanged for thousands of years, as indicated by the bones discovered from different eras.

They have been guardians and protectors of nomads, flocks, villages, and the monasteries of Tibet for hundreds of years. They also have been companions to kings, queens, and presidents, as well as His Holiness the Dalai Lama. Throughout history, the stories reflect their strength, nobility, and intelligence.

Tom was pretty impressed that there were such distinguished animals roaming around the property and was eager to see them again. Judging from the first experience, Sid seemed to be more of a guard dog than Quan was. Maybe he just thought that because Quan was friendlier than Sid was. Anyway, he was glad to have something to tell his grandpa once he returned from his errands.

Tom looked at the armrest of the chair next to him and saw a book opened halfway that his grandpa must have been reading. Tom picked up the book—it was about a guy named Tesla. Nicola Tesla was an inventor of some sort, based upon the description on the back of the book. He flipped through the pages rather quickly. Suddenly a picture caught his eye. He saw a huge pillar with a silver bowl on the top of it. From it emanated several different lightning bolts.

"So, that's where Grandpa learned about throwing lightning," said Tom aloud.

Tom thought perhaps Grandpa wasn't a wizard after all. Maybe he was more of a magician. But that did not explain how he knew about "Waddle." Obviously, there was more to Grandpa than met the eye. Tom grabbed his glass, drank some of the apple juice, and then dove into the Tesla book. This is where his grandpa found him about an hour later.

"Hey there! You're supposed to read about dogs and not about mad scientists," kidded William.

"I did read about the dogs. I knew from history classes that dogs have been around people for a long time, but I didn't think that it would be almost three thousand years ago," said Tom.

"Actually, I think that is a conservative estimate. I think dogs, as a species, have co-existed with man as a valid member of their tribe for even longer. I have seen ancient cave drawings where it shows man hunting with spears and right alongside him were a couple of dogs. It's probably one of the best examples of two different species agreeing to work alongside each other for their mutual benefit." William paused and continued, "That's something you don't see enough of anymore."

"So where did you get Sid and Quan?" asked Tom.

"It's a long story. But to shorten up a bit, I'll tell you that Sid came from China via India, and Quan I found in northern Canada."

William suddenly changed subjects.

"Tom, I want to show you something in the office down here."

Tom nodded and the two of them went to the office. It was a big space, as big as the great room in his house. It had a small desk on one wall with a medium-sized dry erase marker board behind it. There were a couple of chairs with wheels on the bottom so that someone could scoot around as needed. He also noticed something that looked like a padded card table propped up against the far wall.

"Grandpa, do you have a poker table down here?"

William looked puzzled and then saw where Tom was looking. He produced a little grin and answered. "Yup. Lots of poking and prodding goes on atop that table."

The befuddled look on Tom's face made William snort with laughter.

"Tom, it's a massage table when it is put together. It allows you to stretch out and relax on a cushioned surface while someone else pushes and pulls on your body to put it back into alignment."

"Your body can get out of alignment?" asked Tom.

"All the time and in more ways than you know," answered William with a broad grin. "Now have a seat next to the desk, and let me draw you some pictures on the board here."

Tom seated himself and watched his grandpa get out a couple of different colored markers. William pulled a couple of books out from his desk and clapped his hands, turning to Tom. Class was now in session.

"Tom, what is a genius?" asked William.

"A guy who is really smart, I guess," answered Tom.

"Does it only apply to men?"

"OK, a genius is a person who is really smart."

"Better. Now what makes them smarter?" asked William.

"Maybe they had smart parents," offered Tom.

"OK, genetics does play a role in intelligence. But if someone is born from smart parents and if that child never goes to school, chances are not good for him or her to be considered a genius. Therefore, being a genius is a combination of things. It is part genetics—we'll call that Nature."

William went to the board and wrote *Genius?* and then under that wrote *Nature*.

William continued. "It is also partly because of the education of that child, whether by means of schooling, experience, socialization, et cetera. We'll call that Nurture." William wrote that on the board too. As his enthusiasm grew, so, too, did the size of his writing.

"Now we have an idea. Nature and Nurture contribute to how someone becomes a genius. Do you think we have it now or is there something that can prove this statement wrong?"

Tom thought for a bit and then volunteered, "Well, Mark is born from smart people, and he's got schooling and stuff. I think that he has experienced both Nature and Nurture. But I still think that he's a moron!"

William smiled a bit. "Alright then, sibling rivalry aside, I believe you have a valid point. One can have great genes in the family, as well as having a great education and still not be considered a genius." After a brief pause, William continued. "So, who is a genius?"

"Thomas Edison was a genius because he invented the light bulb."

"OK, who else?" asked William.

"Columbus was a genius because he discovered America."

"OK, what about Einstein. Was he a genius?" asked William.

"Yeah, he's a genius because he came up with that formula $E=mc2$."

"Fine. Now, I know that Edison did not even complete elementary school and Einstein dropped out of grade school while in Italy. I also believe that neither one of them came from famous genetic stock. So, how did these ordinary people raise themselves up to the level of genius? What did they do that was so different?"

"Uh, I guess it's because they believed that they could."

"Good! And where do your beliefs come from?" asked William.

"From your mind?" volunteered Tom cautiously.

William smiled, snapped his fingers and did a little dance. "Great answer! These people were not necessarily born with great genes or even had the best teachers. They became geniuses because they learned to use their minds in a different way than most other people do."

"Now answer the following questions: Who discovered America? Who discovered the radio? Who discovered the light bulb?

Here's the tricky part. I do not want you to tell me it was Columbus, Marconi, or Edison."

"Why? Those are the answers I learned in school. OK, I never heard of an inventor named Macaroni, but why should I go looking for answers when the answers are so obvious?"

"You thought it was pretty obvious what was in the woods until Quan and Sid came out, right?"

Tom nodded sheepishly.

"You thought that I was pulling your leg about being a wizard until I read your mind, right?"

Again, Tom nodded. "OK, I get it. Just because I have answers in my head doesn't mean that I was given the correct answers. I should do some thinking on my own."

His grandpa smiled the widest smile he'd ever seen. "Tom, you *are* a genius! You have just realized that you can use your mind differently than most of the people in the world. I have no doubt that someday you will be a better wizard that I am. You are going to get better and better every day."

With that, William stood up, walked to the board, and wrote the word *Gnosis*. He replaced the marker to its ledge and extended his hand to Tom.

"Gnosis?" asked Tom as he took his grandfather's hand.

William did not answer, but smiled with a twinkle in his eye. Grandpa did not let go of Tom's hand. Tom looked questionably up into his grandpa's eyes. William shook Tom's hand a bit more strongly.

"Tom, I am very proud of you. By the end of this week I have no doubt that you will be ready," said William quite sincerely.

"Be ready for what, Grandpa?"

William smiled knowingly and started up the stairs.

"Come on, Tom. Let's get you a decent bedroom and then get to the chores."

Chores? Tom sighed and shuffled after his grandpa. He thought that he had left the concept of chores behind when he left home. Oh, well, how bad could it really be?

With that, he trailed behind his grandpa up the stairs and grabbed his bag of belongings, which was still next to the couch. Tom followed him into the bedroom that was to the left of the fireplace. To the right was William's bedroom.

This bedroom looked more like a normal room because it did not have the high ceiling as the great room had. However, he was surprised to see that the river stone fireplace must have been two sided, because he had a fireplace in his room too.

"That's cool!" said Tom.

"I like it too. I can have a fire in three rooms with one fireplace. However, if you look, this side of the fireplace is tempered glass. If you want to add another log to the fire, you have to do it from the great room."

Tom's gaze continued around the room. Other than a bed, a nightstand, an armoire, a chair, and a desk, the room was free of clutter. A plush Persian rug covered most of the wooden floor in the room.

Tom began unpacking his things into the armoire. He had somewhat hoped to see a TV in there but, unfortunately, it was a true armoire—a place to put clothing.

"There's a pass-through closet into my room through that doorway there. There's a bathroom attached to my bedroom, but you may want to use the one down that hall."

Tom remembered having stumbled into the bathroom after his dad had been in there a while. He was quick to make a mental note that he would take his grandpa's advice and be sure to have his own bathroom. Tom continued to unpack, and his grandpa slipped out of the room. A few minutes later, he came back with a small three-by-five-inch note card. On it was written the following:

Every day, I am getting better and better.

Without saying a word, he placed the card on the corner of the desk in Tom's room and then returned to the doorway.

"When you are finished here, meet me in the barn."

"Are we going to do another experiment?" asked Tom excitedly.

"Something like that," said William.

William headed out to the barn. Before he could even open up the door, along came Tom, running as fast as he could. Together, they pulled open the doors and walked to the primary workbench. William directed Tom to get supplies from different places until the table had a large lantern battery, some wire, a light bulb, a container of salt, a container of water, and an empty jar on it.

William instructed Tom to strip a bit of insulation off the wire and wrap it around both of the battery terminals. He then had Tom wrap one of the wires around one of the sides of the bulb.

"Tom, you notice that when I take the second wire and touch it to the bottom of the bulb ...."

"You complete the circuit and the bulb lights up," finished Tom. "I helped my dad put in additional lights in our barn."

"Good," said William.

William then took a soldering gun from under the workbench and tacked the wires in place on the light bulb. He told Tom that it was just to make sure there was good contact to the bulb. When he finished, he took a pocketknife out and cut one of the wires in half. Immediately, the light went out.

William spoke, "By cutting the wire ...."

"By cutting the wire you have broken the circuit, and now the light won't turn on."

William then stripped the insulation off the ends of the cut wire and handed them to Tom.

"OK, complete the circuit."

Tom touched the ends together and the light came back on again.

"OK, make the light work without touching the wires together."

Tom hesitated for a second. He figured he was supposed to use the water and the salt. Why else would they be sitting there? He grabbed the container of salt and stuck the wires in there. Nothing happened. Maybe the water was the answer. He stuck the wires in the water. Again, nothing happened. Puzzled, he looked to his grandpa.

"Stir a scoop of salt into the container with some water in it, stir it up, and try again," instructed William.

Tom did as he was told and then put the wires back into the water. Inside the bulb, the tiny filament gave off a perceptible orange glow.

"Add more salt?" asked Tom. William nodded.

Tom repeated this process until there was a tiny layer of salt at the bottom of the container; the light had almost completely returned to its previous level of brightness.

"Now think through it very slowly. Visualize the experiment again in your head, and then tell me what just happened," advised William.

Tom gathered his thoughts. He imagined the process over and over in his mind so that he did not forget anything. After a few minutes of visualizing the experiment, he gave his explanation.

"The metal was the best path of electricity, so it made the bulb shine the brightest," said Tom.

"That pathway is called conduction ... the metal is the best conductor of electricity," advised William.

"OK, salt doesn't ... conduct ... electricity because the bulb didn't light up. I always thought that water conducted electricity, but here it didn't. So, I guess water doesn't conduct electricity either. However, once I added the salt to the water, the salt dissolved and the bulb lit. The more salt I added, the brighter the light became. Therefore, saltwater conducts electricity."

"Absolutely fantastic! Your powers of observation are remarkable and will serve you well for the rest of your life. Just remember that you can observe with all of your senses and not just your eyes."

Tom grinned broadly back at his grandpa, but asked him another question. "What happens to the salt when it dissolves?"

"When it dissolves, the salt molecule breaks in half and the resulting elements carry the electricity from one exposed wire to the other. More specifically, true salt is sodium chloride. When in pure water, the bond between the two elements is broken and a slightly positively charged sodium ion is separated from a slightly negatively charged chlorine ion. Negatively charged electrons from the wire travel across the ions to the other exposed wire and complete the circuit, and the bulb lights."

"That was cool, Grandpa. What's next?"

"Next, we tidy up this mess so that we can do another experiment later. Then, we hop into the Jeep. Another adventure awaits!"

Chapter 5 – Landscaping

Once in the Jeep, both Tom and his grandpa were off into the back of his property. A large part of the property was gentle hills and trees of several varieties that presented almost every shade of green. The path they drove on had been cleared so that a vehicle could get through, but the canopy of leaves allowed only speckles of sunlight to make it to the floor. Somewhere in the midst of all the twists and turns, they splashed through a shallow creek. Tom made a mental note to come back here to visit, as it looked quite interesting. Grandpa had to have a fishing pole around somewhere. After a few more minutes of driving, they came to a clearing where some work had already begun.

There were three small trees that had been marked with red ribbon, like that of a Christmas present. Around the bottom of those trees were several wooden stakes. Grandpa stopped the Jeep. He walked around to the back and started pulling out a silver plastic tarp that clanked as if there were heavy tools in it. There were.

"Why are you getting rid of these trees, Grandpa?"

"I'm not getting rid of them. I want to transplant them to the front of the property. There isn't a single silver maple close to the house. So I figured that I would move a couple of them and bring up a walnut tree just to keep them company."

They walked over to the closest tree. It was about twelve feet tall and was very narrow. William took a length of string and tied it around one of the wooden stakes. He went to the next and did the same. Soon, a crude circle surrounded the tree.

"I want to dig a trough around this tree. Try to stay as close to the string as possible. It should be about a foot wide and about two feet deep."

"Grandpa, isn't this a bit too far away from the tree?" asked Tom.

"It may seem that way, but I want to get as many of the roots from the tree as I can. When you move a tree, it needs to have a good-sized root ball so that it will take root at the next location," explained William.

The sounds of shovels and a pickaxe echoed through the woods. Luckily, the ground was soft and the soil did not have any clay. The dirt broke up fairly easily. There was just a lot of it. They dug, and the sounds of the woods started up again. They were serenaded with birdsong, the familiar percussion of a woodpecker, and the occasional frenzy of squirrels scampering through the trees. Although it was a picturesque setting, it was still hard work. After about two hours of digging and hauling dirt away from the site, Tom was exhausted. Sore and drenched in sweat, Tom leaned against his shovel and looked at his grandpa. Grandpa was still going strong, switching back and forth between pickaxe and shovel. Tom looked around to see that only half of the circumscribed area was uncovered.

"Grandpa, I think you need to stick me with a fork because I'm done."

William chuckled and glanced up to see his grandson looking as if he had taken his T-shirt right out of the wash, kicked it around in the dirt for a few minutes, and put it on. Dirt was smudged on his face, hands, and forearms. *No matter what anyone thinks, Tom certainly gets into his work*, thought William. Not wanting to wear him out on his first day, William agreed.

"OK, we're done here. Let's get the tools under the tarp, and we'll leave them here until tomorrow."

"We're going to be back here tomorrow?" asked Tom. He was already thinking of sore muscles that had not yet begun to hurt.

"Yes, I want to work out here a little bit every day. The more work we can get done before it rains, the better off we'll be."

"Working in the rain would stink," surmised Tom.

"Not just that, the rain will gather in the hole and make the soil denser and harder to work with later," added William.

"I guess that would stink too ... about as much as I do now," said Tom.

"I don't know if that is possible," said William with his lopsided grin.

Tom pretended to smell his armpit and then staggered for two or three steps. Both of them had a good laugh as they began to tidy up the area.

Tom took his shovel as well as his grandpa's and put them under the tree. He then took the tarp and covered up the tools. Grandpa found a few rocks and put them on the tarp to make sure that it didn't blow away. Once they were both satisfied, they headed toward the Jeep. They were naming things that stink and were making each other laugh when they heard a steady thump in the back of the Jeep. Quan's tail was letting them know where she was hiding. As they walked up to the Jeep, the thumping became stronger and the tips of her ears were seen just above the back seat.

"Quan, have you been spying on us?" asked William.

Quan's head popped up and a single woof answered in the affirmative. Tom reached over the side of the Jeep and scratched her head and ears with both hands. Still, the tail kept a steady beat. William walked to the driver side of the vehicle, got in, started the motor, and then turned around.

"Quan, show me the way home," said William.

Quan scrambled out of the back of the vehicle, trotted about fifty feet away, and stopped. Tom jumped in, and, once they started moving, Quan trotted down the hill and followed the same path they originally took to get back there. She knew to take a route that they could follow. She continued to lead them back toward the house. Once it was in sight, she galloped to the garage door and waited.

When they got inside the garage, Quan sat down next to a refrigerator that William had for extra storage. Her tail dusted the floor with anticipation. William unlocked the refrigerator door, opened it, and then threw a thick slice of ham to Quan. Quan caught it in midair and gobbled it down. She watched to see if there would be another piece coming. William closed the door and locked it again. Once she saw the door being locked, she turned and walked over to Tom to be petted again.

"I had to put a lock on the door because she figured out how to open it when no one was around. Having smart companions keeps you on your toes, that's for sure."

"She is definitely the smartest dog I have ever seen," said Tom.

"Well, go get your shower and then we'll grab a late lunch."

Tom showered, put on some fresh clothes and then met his grandpa in the kitchen. Grandpa, looking freshly scrubbed, had put out a tray of freshly cut vegetables, hummus, tabouli, and pita bread. Tom was mortified. He took one look at the hummus and thought it looked like a mixture of butterscotch pudding and baby poop. He snickered at the thought briefly; disgust returned when he realized that he would have to eat this stuff.

"Grandpa, why in the world do you eat all this weird stuff?" asked Tom as he sat down.

"Why do you call this stuff weird? Would you like to know what really goes into a hot dog? Snouts and ears ... now that's weird eating," responded William waving a wooden spoon at him.

William continued putting things on the table for the meal. Every time he cast a glance at Tom, he looked like a he'd been on a carnival ride a bit too long. Finally, he sat down and looked intently at his grandson.

"Tom, what is your favorite thing in the world to eat?"

"Is this another experiment, Grandpa?"

"It is an experiment in a way. I am going to get you to use the limitless power of your mind," said William.

"If my mind was limitless then I would be imagining a machine that turns this yucky stuff into a hamburger and french fries," grinned Tom.

"OK, we'll try that later. Right now is now. Now, I want you to tell me what is your favorite food in the whole world?"

"Warm brownies with nuts right out of the oven. Why? Do you have any brownies?" asked Tom hopefully. Who knew ... he could read minds. He could make brownies too.

"No, no brownies. What I want you to do is close your eyes and imagine a huge clock. A clock with a face ... not a digital clock," said William.

"Like that clock in England ... Big Ben?"

"Well, the bell's name is Big Ben, but yes, just like that," said William.

Tom closed his eyes. He opened one of them just to be sure that his grandpa wasn't trying to offer him a bite of hummus and tell him it was cookie dough.

"Now, now, now," chastised William.

"OK, I see it."

"Fine," said William. "Now imagine, in vivid detail, that you have a big, warm, yummy brownie. I want you to put it on the face of that clock somewhere. Anywhere will do."

Tom could imagine the brownie with walnut chunks oozing out the side. The warmth of the brownie caused it to reveal a wisp of steam. The smell of brownies filled the air. Tom's imagination was so intense that he was salivating.

"OK, it's on the clock," said Tom in a reverent tone.

"Great. Now tell me, where on the face of the clock is it?" inquired William.

"It's on the six o'clock position," answered Tom.

"Fine. Now I want you to imagine where you would put a bowl of hummus and a bowl of tabouli."

Tom's answer was immediate.

"On the twelve o'clock position. As far away from the brownie as I could get it."

"Alright then," William grinned, "I want you to imagine that you are going to take the brownie off of the face of the clock and then you are going to put the bowls of hummus and tabouli in its place."

"Can I just eat the brownie?" asked Tom wistfully.

"No," chuckled William, "you just need to set it aside and move the bowls as I told you."

Mentally, Tom made the brownie vanish and the bowls slide down the clock to the six o'clock position.

"OK, they are in place," said Tom.

"Wonderful, we're almost done. I want you to imagine that you have a big hammer and some really strong nails. You are going to imagine that you nail the bowls to that position. You will not break the bowls, and the nails will drive completely into the face of the clock," instructed William.

"Can I pretend that I am actually nailing them?" asked Tom.

"An excellent suggestion. Keep your eyes closed, but you go ahead and nail the heck out of those suckers."

Tom's smile spread across his face as he began mimicking the act of hammering a nail. With his eyes closed, he swung his imaginary hammer and gave the nail several determined blows. So great was his ferocity that his tongue stuck out of his mouth a bit as if to assist in the matter. William couldn't help but laugh out loud. He could not decide if he was more amazed at his grandson's intensity or his imagination.

"OK, Grandpa," said Tom as he dropped his hands to his lap, "I nailed them really good. They aren't going anywhere."

"Alright then, let's eat!"

Tom's eyes popped open. The same food as before was there, but for some reason the thought of baby poop did not come to his mind. Instead he thought that he smelled garlic in the hummus. He really liked garlic. It wouldn't be too awful. He took several pieces of the quartered pita bread and then scooped a little hummus and tabouli onto his plate. He had a glass of water close by, just in case. He nudged a corner of the pita bread into the hummus and held it up to his nose. It didn't smell bad. Finally, he summoned the courage to take a bite. He was so shocked that his whole body tingled.

"Grandpa, this stuff is really good! Why didn't you tell me that beforehand?"

"I could have, but you needed to decide that for yourself. I just needed to show you how to approach it. You see, the mind is the most powerful tool that we have in this world. You can achieve anything in the world if you set your mind to it. No matter if it is learning a difficult subject in school, dealing with people who get on your nerves, or eating something that you might think is icky. Once you decide that something is going to be a certain way, then it will probably be that way. Don't put limitations on yourself or on your expectations. You may be surprised at what you discover," said William.

As William was speaking, he was looking in Tom's general direction but he was not really looking at him. When he stopped talking and really looked at Tom, he noticed that Tom had already finished what he had served himself and was going back for a substantially larger portion than before.

"Uh-oh, looks like I may have to put a lock on this refrigerator too," smiled William.

"It's really good," said Tom around a mouthful of food. He smiled and kept eating one of his new favorite foods.

Chapter 6 – Explorers

Over lunch they discussed the placement of the trees, how long it would take to get the trees out of the ground, the lightning experiment, and the Tibetan mastiffs. So much had gone on in only his first day that Tom had to take time to go through it all again just to be sure that he had not forgotten anything. As it turned out, he had. However, his grandpa was there to make sure that wasn't the case for very long. After they finished lunch, they went to the great room, plopped down on the couch, and gazed absently at the fireplace. Tom was first to interrupt the silence.

"How do you do it, Grandpa?"

"How do I do what?"

"How is it that you know so much? I mean I know that you're old and ... well, I don't mean that in a bad way. It's just that ... that older people have been around longer and that's why they have more knowledge."

Tom paused for a moment and then continued. "Some people say that you can't teach an old dog new tricks, but that does not seem to apply to you. Why?"

William paused and took a drink of water. "I think what I have in common with people my age is that I have felt tired, old, weak, confused, and depressed at one time or another. I just never felt any of that for too long; those are the old dogs I didn't want to feed and keep around, in a manner of speaking."

William nodded his head as though he heard another definition and then said, "I'd like to believe it is because I never decided to give up. Some of the people that I used to hang out with got tired of learning. Maybe it is more precise to say that they got tired of trying to learn. It was almost as if they decided that at a certain age they would just stop collecting knowledge. I have never felt that way."

William stared out the window overlooking the back of his property. He watched the trees sway gently back and forth in the breeze to collect his thoughts. He concluded, "I have never felt that I had learned enough."

Tom rolled that over in his mind. It dawned on him that Grandpa was not just "Grandpa." He was a person just like him. They both liked to read, to experiment, to follow their curiosity, and to do the things they liked to do regardless of what others thought of them. Grandpa wasn't just some old fart who showed up for meals occasionally. He was a smart and creative dude who didn't brag about what he knew or did. He was a wizard who didn't show off.

"Have you always been able to read people's minds?" asked Tom.

"No, that is a power of mind that I have developed over a number of years."

"Where did you learn something like that?" asked Tom.

"Tom, all the things that you will ever want to know will eventually make their way to you. I will help you as much as I can. However, I won't answer that question on this ... on your first day."

"Will you tell me before I leave?" asked Tom.

"Yes, before you leave you will know where I learned something like that," said William carefully.

They returned to sitting in silence. William continued to stare out into the woods while the trees swayed to a gentle lullaby that came from the air itself. Tom continued to look around the room at the little trinkets and souvenirs from various places Grandpa had visited. Suddenly, Tom had a great idea.

"Can you guess lottery numbers or baseball scores?" asked Tom.

"You know, I have never tried. If I had to guess, I would say probably it wouldn't work because I would not be working for the highest good. I would be working for my own personal good. When you attempt to be self-serving, the Universe tends to block you," responded William.

"What else can you do?" asked Tom.

"Some of that will be revealed tomorrow. For now, I want you to go down to the library and get working on those obvious questions that won't be so obvious," said William.

Remembering that he was supposed to question the answers to questions that everyone should know, Tom agreed. He picked up his glass of water and made his way to the top of the stairs. He turned to look at his grandpa.

"Thanks, Grandpa."

William smiled at Tom. He raised his glass as if to give a toast.

Tom returned the salute and headed down to the basement library.

It was late in the afternoon, but the modified skylights still gave a lot of light to the library. Once again, he began wandering around, waiting for a book to jump out at him. There were so many to choose from that it was all still a bit imposing. However, he perused the shelves and waited for something to catch his eye. The first thing that caught his attention wasn't a book at all; it was a really big seashell. It was easily twice the size of the palm of Tom's hand. It was pretty cool looking because it had a rainbow of iridescent colors on the inside. Lying inside the shell was a small stick that had some string tied around it.

Looking at the stick closer, he realized that it was really a bunch of very small twigs and tiny plants that had been dried. It had a silver green color. When Tom smelled it, he knew that it was the source of the pleasant smoky odor he had noticed when he was down here the first time. Knowing his grandpa, Tom knew it was something that he had grown, dried, and made himself. He would have to remember to ask him what this was later.

Tom walked to the office and grabbed a pen and some paper. He returned to looking for a book on questioning common knowledge. He wandered around until a series of books finally grabbed his attention. It was a set of encyclopedias from 2002. He pulled out the third book and looked up Christopher Columbus. As he read, he jotted down some notes. When he came across an interesting fact, he jotted that down, too, but he printed it in capital letters so that he could organize his thoughts later. There were a few things that Tom was sure about Columbus, and his research confirmed them. Columbus was a well-established sailor prior to making his epic journey to the New World. He had made numerous trips along the trade routes close to Spain. What was shocking to Tom was the fact that Columbus had been a slave trader! This meant that Columbus also knew the trade routes to and from Africa. Tom wondered how many people would celebrate Columbus Day if they knew his fame was due to the suffering of others. Tom also knew that Columbus' discoveries were due, in part, to the fact that new trade routes to India were desirable. What he didn't know was new trade routes were necessary because the city of Constantinople was taken over by the Turks. Several trade routes passed through this huge city. The route to the Indies (India, China, and Japan) was motivated by greed, not exploration.

Another motivation for Columbus was pride. There would be enormous bragging rights if he found this alternative route to the Indies. If discovered, it would probably be named after him. To become such a famous navigator and explorer, he would probably be elevated to the level of aristocracy. Tom discovered that this fact meant more than fame. This meant that he would be able to pass on his properties and holdings down through the generations.

So when the city of Constantinople was taken over in 1453, a new route to the Indies was on the minds of many. A route around the southern tip of Africa was known but used sparingly, as the route was extremely dangerous. Yet the drive to get to the Indies was constant. The spices from this region of the world were used for more than

63

seasoning. They were also used for money and medicine.

Columbus was a driven man. He came up with a plan to approach the Indies from the west and proposed this plan to both businessmen and royalty. Although born in Italy, Columbus proposed his ideas to the powers that existed at that time—Spain and Portugal. Both countries turned down his idea for the same reasons. Both royal courts believed that Columbus underestimated the cost of the voyage and the length of the trip.

In fact, Columbus was in error in several areas. He did underestimate the length of the trip because he underestimated the circumference of the Earth by twenty-five percent. He also mistakenly believed that the Earth was comprised mostly of land. Finally, some researchers say he didn't know about the two continental landmasses blocking his way. Still, Columbus persisted, and in 1492, the Spanish royal court finally gave in and gave him permission to sail forth.

Columbus, an accomplished mapmaker, navigator, and sailor, was boldly going where, supposedly, no one had gone before. As such, the first voyage took seventy days. (Subsequent trips went as fast as twenty-one days!) Columbus never did find a way to the Indies, but he did find several of the Caribbean islands. Oddly enough, he never did find North America. The closest he ever came was Puerto Rico.

The native people that Columbus first discovered called themselves the Tainos. Columbus referred to them as "savages" in his personal journals. However, they were not. They knew how to process and weave cotton, their villages were laid out in an organized manner, and they had both social and governmental systems. Historians have been debating that the word "savage" was a code word meaning that they could be made into slaves.

Columbus, as well as most of the other Europeans, was not kind to the Tainos. In fact, Columbus was cruel to them. Columbus made all of the male Tainos over fourteen years old look for gold. Those who did not make their quota of gold were beaten, whipped, and, in some cases, had their hands cut off. Any Tainos who protested this treatment became slaves.

Tom stopped writing and paused to think about what he had learned so far. It seemed strange to him that the United States would have a national holiday celebrating someone who traded slaves and allowed such vicious behavior toward the Tainos. There had to be some good in this story somewhere. Tom returned to the book and began looking for where the good things had been hiding.

Tom discovered that the contact between the two worlds resulted in increased trade in items like cotton, rubber, sugar cane, furs, precious metals, chocolate, hot peppers, peanuts, and tomatoes. Europe returned the favor by supplying the New World with cattle, goats, honey bees, horses, sheep, pigs, rice, and other plants.

The downside to this exchange was that the crops needed a lot of care. Therefore, the demand for slaves increased. The separation of Europeans and Indians also separated certain diseases. Malaria, measles, small pox, tetanus, and typhus swept through the native populations and killed vast numbers of native people. In turn, the

Europeans were exposed to a form of syphilis that had been previously unknown.

To put it simply, Columbus should be admired for his persistence, courage, and sailing abilities. He should also be despised for his cruelty toward the Tainos, his slave trading, and his contribution toward exploiting natural resources.

Tom leaned back in his chair and reread his report to be sure he liked it. Suddenly, he sat upright as he realized he had not answered an important question—who discovered America?

Further research really surprised him. Columbus discovered parts of South America in the 1490s. Another Italian sailor, John Cabot, discovered the most northern part of North America of Nova Scotia and Newfoundland. Some say that Amerigo Vespucci discovered the North American continent, but the supporting documents have been altered at some point. As it happens, the Vikings originally discovered North America around 1000. *Maybe this continent should be called Norse America*, thought Tom.

Chapter 7 – Communication

Tom put down his pen. He folded his hands and then rested his head on the table. All of the effort put into research made him ready to take a break. As he dozed off, he dreamt that he was in the woods behind the house. He was wandering around and trying to find his bearings. He listened for Quan's familiar bark but only heard the birds in the trees chattering back and forth. He discovered a path that he instinctively knew as a deer trail. As he was walking along this trail, he spied a young man leaning against a tree as though he had been waiting.

He appeared to be about the same age as Tom. He was dressed only in buckskin pants and moccasins. His round smiling face was framed with hair so black that it looked almost dark violet in the sunlight. Tom was not startled to see another person in the woods with him. In fact, he was starting to leave his mind open to just about anything where his grandpa, or this place, was concerned.

They stood and stared at each other for a second. Tom found his voice first.

"Uh, hi there," said Tom.

"Hi," said the other boy.

"I'm Tom. What's your name?"

"I have many names. You can call me Little Eagle."

"Can you tell me how to find my grandpa?" asked Tom.

"He will find you first," answered Little Eagle.

With that Little Eagle pointed down the path and nodded in that direction. Tom looked down the wooded path and saw nothing but more trees. When he turned to ask Little Eagle what he had seen, Little Eagle had disappeared.

Tom felt that he was supposed to find something along the path, although he could not say what it was. Still, he kept looking. Suddenly, as if someone had turned off a light switch, it became dark in the woods. Tom realized that he was really lost. He tried to find his way in the dark and heard dogs barking; he stood still to hear where the sounds were coming from. The echo did not provide a direction, but the dogs were getting closer. He could only hope that it was Quan or Sid coming to get him.

"Tom, are you going to sleep here all night?" asked William.

His grandpa's voice finally seeped into his consciousness. Tom raised his head and looked at him with a groggy, vacant stare. He blinked a few times and then looked at him directly.

"I was lost in the woods. The dogs were coming to get me," said Tom.

"Well, you're here in the library now. You are probably hearing Sid and Quan out by the garage door. They know that I feed them at sunset."

"Wow, it's sunset already?"

"Yes, sir," said William in a humorous tone. "It happens about this time of day every day."

With a pat on the back from his grandpa, Tom got up and followed William out to the garage to feed the dogs. Meeting Little Eagle in the dream was forgotten—for the time being. As they walked out to the garage, Tom felt he had something he should be telling his grandpa, but he couldn't put a finger on it. They walked in silence to the waiting diners.

The menu that evening was probably the best that any dog could have wished for. It was almost all food that Tom would have eaten. Grandpa explained that Tibetan mastiffs did not tolerate normal dog food very well. In fact, they did not do well on grains that comprise most dog food. Sid and Quan were fed a mix of a special type of hard dog food, along with a can of wet dog food. On top of this went a few slices of luncheon meat and an egg.

"My friends here are a bit more difficult to keep around because of their dietary restrictions. You just can't feed them a bag of Joe Bob's dog food and not expect them to feel bad," commented William.

Tom just stared at his grandpa with a lopsided grin on his face and waited.

"On the other hand, they are my family and I want to treat them the best way I know how," concluded William begrudgingly.

"Don't you feel bad knowing your dogs eat better than some people?" asked Tom.

"It wouldn't be any different if I had kids. In fact, the dogs have less of an impact on the planet than humans do. I also donate a bit of money to a few different charities," stated William. He paused for a few seconds.

"I try to live in such a way that if I discover I have caused an imbalance in the world, then I do something to counterbalance it," asserted William.

"We talked about this in science class ... about how each person has a carbon footprint. We spent a while figuring out how we can create a smaller footprint," remembered Tom.

"Our family was doing pretty good since we are on a well system, we have rain barrels, we recycle and replaced our light bulbs. Dad wants to install a wind turbine ... says it would look like it belongs there since we live in a farmhouse."

William replied, "Your dad does a good job these days trying to keep in balance. The American Indians and the Tibetan monks you saw pictures of in my hallway knew how to be in balance in many aspects of life. Speaking of balance, your parents haven't seen or heard from you in almost a whole day. They will probably be wondering about you since I whisked you away from home in such an unceremonious fashion. While I put together something for dinner, why don't you give them a call and let them know how you're doing."

"OK," responded Tom.

Tom went back through the basement and into the classroom. On the desk was the portable phone. The word *Gnosis* stared at Tom. He made a mental reminder to ask Grandpa about this later. Tom grabbed the phone and went to the patio where all the different herbs were growing. The setting sun had left pastel colors on the skyline—just like the smell of perfume after a woman has left the room, there was a lingering presence to remind you of her radiance. Tom admired the sky for a few seconds longer before he plopped down in a comfortable chair and phoned his parents.

"Hello?" answered Karen.

"Hi, Mom. How are you?" asked Tom through a wide grin.

"I'm good, Tommy. The question is how are you? You both rushed off before we could give you a proper goodbye," said Karen enthusiastically.

"I'm fine. Grandpa said you would say that. He has got some really cool stuff out here at the cabin. Did you know that?" asked Tom.

"I knew that your grandpa really liked the place. I was out there once when Mark was about three years old. I was very pregnant with you at the time so I didn't get to look around the cabin too much. Did he ever finish his basement?" asked Karen.

"Yup. He built that and then some," answered Tom.

Tom continued in detail, describing the cabin she had not seen in several years. The cabin's basement, the underground garage, and the tunnel to the barn were all new to her. In fact, the description of the grounds surprised both of them. From what Karen remembered, there were not too many trees from the roadway to the house. Tom described it filled with pine trees and wild flowers. He also described the process of moving trees from the far end of the property to the front of the property. Karen thought that it was good that a carpenter would spend so much time restoring the woods. Still, she still thought of the place as William's "man space."

Since his dad and brother were not around, Tom continued talking to his mom and told her of all the experiments and the research he had done thus far. He even told her about the experiment they did with the hummus. Karen was quite surprised to hear that her young son craved hummus almost as much as brownies.

Once all there was to say was said, Tom bid his mom good-bye and said that he would talk to her later. Karen gave him a kiss through the phone and said that she would miss him until he called again. Before she hung up with Tom, she had one piece of advice.

"Be sure to pay attention to your grandpa at all times. He has a sneaky habit of teaching you things when you don't even realize it," said Karen, smiling into the phone.

Dinner was uneventful as Tom recognized it as a pan of lasagna. There was no need to imagine this on a clock since Tom liked lasagna very much. Grandpa mixed up some olive oil with a few different herbs he had drying on a shelf in the kitchen so they would have something to dip their bread into during dinner. The hard rolls, still warm from the oven, were a great complement to the dinner. The conversation over dinner dealt mostly with the discussion Tom had with his mother and reviewing the experiences of the day. Once dinner was over and the dishes cleared away, the two of them went for a walk down the driveway path to the road.

As they walked out the front door, Sid and Quan came bounding around the corner of the house, sped past them, and then kept track of them, darting in and out of the tree line. Although it was very dark out this far from a city, the moonlight still showed the path to the roadway. Tom began thinking about the morning and asked his grandpa what the next day's agenda was going to be.

"Tomorrow I am going to give you a little history on me and how I became a wizard. To be more precise, I will tell you how I became an alchemist ... a person who craves knowledge and spiritual enlightenment simultaneously. I will also tell you how you can discover your own mind's potential and how best to develop it and use it in day to day life," answered William.

"How long ago was this, Grandpa?"

William picked up a handful of small rocks from the roadway and began flicking them from his hand one by one. A light evening breeze gently tussled his hair.

"This was back in the early seventies, if I remember correctly. I started this journey to become more knowledgeable about self-hypnosis and to manage stress. I quickly discovered that the longer I practiced the techniques, the better I became at using them. As I got better at the traditional techniques, I went back to learn more esoteric or unusual ones. People I met wanted to learn more. Eventually, I taught these techniques as a class to others."

"So, how long did it take for you to become psychic?" asked Tom.

"Tom, I became psychic by the end of my very first class. I was reading medical case studies of people who had volunteered their medical history and written it on a document I had never seen. I could know their physical ailments and their personality traits, and I could know if there was a problem coming up for them. The more that I used my psychic abilities, the stronger and more refined they became," answered William.

Tom was taking all of this in as best he could. Even in the moonlight, he could see that his grandpa was watching him intently to see if what he had said made sense. William decided to use a different analogy.

"Imagine that your brain is a computer. I want to defragment your hard drive and upgrade your operating system to a better and more stable environment. Once we do that, we will look for any bugs in your programming. We will not patch ... we will replace any defective files and then run some benchmarking tests to see if we are better than our previous build and specifications," said William.

They walked in silence a few seconds longer before Tom spoke.

"Grandpa, you never cease to amaze me. I didn't know that you knew all that computer stuff," exclaimed Tom.

William just smiled in the dark. He put his arm around Tom's neck and they walked back to the warmly lit house where a nice comfortable bed would be waiting for each of them. Quan led the way.

Tom ambled to the bathroom and got ready for bed. Once back in his bedroom, he tossed his dirty clothes onto the desk. It was then that he noticed the small note card his grandpa had placed there earlier that day. He paused long enough to read it out loud.

"Every day, I am getting better and better."

Yawning mightily, he flopped into bed and put the note card next to him on the nightstand. He pulled up the sheet and covers and was almost asleep when his head hit the pillow. Before he drifted off, he noticed that the heat pump in the basement made a pleasant hum in his room. Although he would not remember it the next morning, he spent most of his sleep running through the woods playing hide and seek with his new friend Little Eagle.

Chapter 8 – Culture Shock

The next morning was a bit disorienting for Tom. The first thing he thought about was coffee. Since his dad made coffee every morning, he felt as if he were at home. Finally, he opened his eyes and stared at a wall that had a fireplace sticking out of it. His new reality washed over him as he remembered that he was still at his grandpa's house in the woods. He sprang from the bed, quickly dressed, and went out to meet his grandpa. Today was the day that the mystery of how Grandpa became a wizard ... psychic ... alchemist ... would be revealed.

As he came out of his room, he was a bit disappointed. Although he did not know what to expect, he did not expect to see just another average day. Grandpa was sitting at the kitchen table with a cup of steaming coffee in his hand and a magazine in front of him. Grandpa was wearing jeans and a T-shirt with two cartoon characters on it. It was quite faded and worn but he could still make out the name Astrix. The characters of a very small and a very big Viking looked at him with grinning faces but offered no explanation.

A wicker basket with a red and white checked towel hiding a mound of something sat in the middle of the table. It was hard to tell if it had any aroma because the smell of coffee was overwhelming. William looked up from his magazine and smiled.

"Ah, *guten Morgen*, Thomas! *Schlafs gut, ja?*"

"Huh?" responded Tom.

"GU-ten ... MOR-gan ...," said William again.

"Uh ... good morning?" asked Tom.

"Ja!" said William. "Schlaf's gut?"

"Did I sleep good?" asked Tom.

"Ja! Guten Morgen. Schlaf's gut?" asked William.

"Sehr gut. Danke," said Tom.

"Ausgeignet!" said William. "Where did you learn to speak German?"

"I don't speak German, Grandpa. I just know a couple of words from TV," said Tom.

"TV!" said William incredulously. "Since when do they teach German on TV?"

"Well, I learned some from watching Harrison Ford and Bruce Willis movies. I learned more by watching a show on late at night called *Hogan's Heroes*," answered Tom.

"Well, I guess TV isn't a complete wasteland," replied William.

"So why were you speaking to me in German? When did you start?" asked Tom.

"Well, I was thinking in German at the time, so I thought I would surprise you with it. Many years ago, when I was younger, I dated a girl named Ute who was from Switzerland. She did not speak very much English. I did not speak German or French so I decided to learn a little of each," said William.

"She spoke French too?" asked Tom.

"Oh, yes. Driving across two or three states here is like driving through two or three countries in Europe. The need to speak a couple of different languages is quite prevalent in Europe. Also, the ability to practice your language skills is as easy as going for a short drive. In fact, most countries teach their mother tongue, English or Russian, and another language, all while still in elementary school," said William.

He paused to sip his coffee and continued, "Funny that our country can barely teach its youth one language."

Tom grabbed a cup of coffee; a hard roll left over from the night before and some marmalade and sat adjacent to his grandfather. They drank decaffeinated coffee at home, so having coffee with breakfast did not bother Tom.

"German is a hard language to learn isn't it?" asked Tom.

"Oh, no. Absolutely not. Many of the words we use in English are Germanic. *Kome* means come, *sitz* means sit, *stehe* means stay, *halt* means stop, *werk* means work, *bier* means beer, *haus* means house ... trust me, Tom, there are a lot of similarities," said William.

"If it's such a similar language, how come they don't teach it to us in school?" asked Tom.

William just smiled back at Tom and nodded as though he agreed. He then looked down at Tom's plate and saw what he was getting ready to eat. He also saw what he was getting ready to drink. With a grin, he just sat and watched out of the corner of his eye while he resumed flipping through his *Stern* magazine.

Tom went to stir a spoonful of sugar into his coffee and noticed that it was slightly brown. He touched a bit to his tongue and discovered that it tasted like regular sugar. He added in some cream from the refrigerator and then took a sip.

"Holy crap! Grandpa, how much coffee did you put into the coffeemaker this morning!" exclaimed Tom.

William chuckled in a deep, hearty fashion.

"There is a saying that coffee should be dark as night, sweet as love, and strong as death," said William.

"Well, you've definitely got that formula right!" exclaimed Tom.

"There's a coffee for every taste, Tom. I get my beans from a company called Green Mountain coffee. Met the owner ... wonderful man ... great business ethic. Anyway, I grind up my beans only when I want to use them. That way they stay fresh. Then you decide how strong you want it. For example, you are drinking what I would call café Cubano. It is *mucho robusto!*"

"Grandpa, you could stain a table with that coffee," muttered Tom.

William continued chuckling. He got up and took Tom's coffee to the sink. He drank almost half of it and filled it back up with hot water. He then added another scoop of sugar and a dash of cream. He handed it back to Tom.

"Try this."

"I like this a heck of a lot better," said Tom.

"Well, Tom, in your travels outside the United States, make sure you ask for café Americano," replied William. "Also, before you break your teeth on that hard roll, have a look in the basket."

Tom pulled lack the layers of towel and discovered raspberry and blueberry muffins. They were huge ... so much so that one muffin filled his entire hand. The brown sugar and butter had crystallized across the top and under that was the best muffin he had ever seen.

"Wow, Grandpa, you can really cook! Mom's doesn't even come close," said Tom.

"Well, I can't take the credit for these. I have some neighbors toward the north who asked permission to come onto my property and pick raspberries, blueberries, and walnuts. I told them to help themselves as long as they bring me a sample of whatever they make from them every so often. I get muffins and pies in the summer and jams in the fall," explained William.

Soon Tom had eaten three muffins and finished his reconstructed coffee. William finished perusing his magazine and sat sipping his coffee quietly while waiting for Tom to finish eating. Finally, Tom sat back from his plate and deeply sighed with content. He looked at his grandpa for a second and shared what was on his mind.

"You know, when I got up this morning, I thought it looked like a pretty boring morning ... kind of like any other. But so far, I've had a conversation in German, you were reading a German magazine, and I got a lesson in how foreign countries teach their kids and how they drink their coffee. The way things appear are not how they really are sometimes," said Tom.

"Tom, you are *so* ready to learn what I am about to teach you," said William with a big smile.

"So ... let's get started!" said Tom.

"Indeed," said William as he stood up and headed for the stairs. Tom followed almost at a gallop.

Chapter 9 – Gnosis

Once again they were in William's downstairs classroom. Class was now in session. William pulled a crisp notebook from his desk drawer and handed it and a pen to Tom as he took a seat. Grabbing a marker, William went to the dry erase board and wrote the following:

How to Become a Gnostic—Mental Discipline
Overview
Science of the Mind/Brain
Training Format
    Relaxation
    NLP
    Self-improvement
    ESP

"Tom, here is where we begin your gnostic training. The first thing I want you know is that none of this is magic, spooky, or bad. None of this requires special schooling. It does not require you to change your religion, leave your family, or spend hours and hours learning about herbology, mythology, or any other '-ology.' What it requires is a belief that all of the capabilities and possibilities we will talk about are attainable. All it requires is an open mind and a willingness to be open to your own talents that have been dormant.

"What I want to focus on today is your open-ended growth, rather than reshaping your personality to conform to the expectations of society. At any point in our training, my aim is to stimulate your self-enlightenment, self-awareness, and self-development. Someday, when you study psychology, pay particular attention to humanistic psychology. Or, simply put, I want you to become the best 'you' that you can be."

William paused again to give Tom a chance to catch up with his note taking. He went to the garage, grabbed a couple of bottles of water, and returned to the classroom. He left a bottle on Tom's desk and opened the other. He pulled on the back of his T-shirt for some slack and leaned against the front of the desk. After a long drink from the bottle he looked at Tom. Tom's thirst had nothing to do with water.

"Let's talk a bit about the science of the brain," William continued. "The brain is an organ of the body and is similar to the heart. The heart has electrical impulses. So does the brain. The heart beats so many times per second based upon the activity being performed. So too, the brain. The beats, or cycles, of the heart can be measured by a device called the electrocardiogram or ECG, sometimes called an EKG. The brain's activity can be measured much the same way by a similar device called an electroencephalogram, also known as an EEG.

"Scientists in brain research follow the model passed on by Hans Berger developed in the nineteen twenties. It names beta waves as those brain frequencies above fourteen cycles per second—called

CPS; alpha waves are those at seven to fourteen CPS; theta waves are at four to seven CPS; and delta waves are one-half to four CPS."

Tom scribbled as fast as he could to keep up with the flow of information. As Tom put down his pen and stretched the muscles of his hand, William began again.

"Research tells us that during a twenty-four-hour period, people generally experience each one of these cycles. Research also indicates that when the brain shows beta waves on an EEG, a person is in full consciousness or awareness. When the brain shows alpha waves, the person has muted the external world, is physically still, and is in a state similar to meditation. When the brain shows theta waves, the person has withdrawn from nearly all external stimulation and is usually asleep. When the brain shows delta waves, the person is totally unconscious, that is, unaware of themselves and their environment."

William paused to give Tom time to catch up. Once he did, Tom looked up at William.

"Go through your notes thus far and tell me if there are any gaps or if there is anything that you have a question about," said William.

Tom started at the top of his notes and read through them. In a couple of places he added a word or two for clarification. After he got to the bottom of his notes, he looked to his grandpa.

"The only question I have so far is that you have used the word *brain* and the word *mind* in your outline. What is the difference between the two? Is there a difference?" asked Tom.

"Again, Thomas, you are proving yourself to be a genius because you are asking questions that have tickled the intellect of philosophers and scientists for centuries."

William turned to the board and wrote:

Cognita ergo summa Or Summa ergo cognita

"I think, therefore I am .... or ... I am, therefore I think," said William as he set his marker down.

"I will borrow from Plato and answer your question with a question. Do human beings have a soul?" asked William.

"Yeah, we have souls, like spirits, right? I mean both Mom and Dad are always saying that we are spiritual beings having a physical experience," said Tom.

"OK, if we have souls, where is the soul organ?" asked William.

"I don't know," said Tom honestly.

"Exactly. There is not a soul organ on any anatomy chart, but lots of people believe we have a soul. There are others who believe we are soulless. There are still others who believe we are not even really here on Earth but are living inside of a cosmic video game."

Tom shook his head as though he were trying to get a spider out of his hair. Suddenly, he had a flash of insight.

"Just like the movie *The Matrix*," said Tom.

85

"Yes, I believe we are all a part of a matrix of sorts," said William thoughtfully. "I am going to explain this as best as I can, but I am sure there are others who will

explain this to you more completely."

William chuckled to himself as if he were remembering something amusing, walked over to the board, and wrote the following:

thought   *connection*   *action*

He drew lines from the words and then connected the following three words:

mind   brain   muscle

"Let's say your mind has a thought." William wrote on the board:

I have no idea what hummus is.

"Almost instantaneously your brain will have an emotional connection to the thought ... like displeasure or negativity." He continued writing.

Hummus is a weird word to me. It must be yucky.

"After having the brain attach an emotion to the mind's thought, your brain tells the body to spring to action."

You push the hummus away and do not eat any because it is in the yucky file.

"So, what happened to you?" asked William while twirling the marker in his fingers.

"Well, I guess you changed my mind—or my brain. You had me imagine the hummus and the brownie. You had me think about how good the brownie would be when I ate it. So I did what you told me and then I liked it," said Tom.

"Yes, that's correct. But allow me to elaborate. You changed your own mind; I just showed you a path to achieve it. Your brain has a file on brownies. It can form a picture of one when only the word is mentioned. It has also associated an emotional response to brownies. You love brownies, right?" asked William.

"Oh, yeah!" said Tom.

"You also have a physical response. When I talk about brownies, your mouth begins to water, right?"

"Yeah," answered Tom, now getting hungry.

"OK, so now you saw this new brown mushy stuff. I called it hummus. Your brain then opened a file called *hummus* and the picture of the brown mushy stuff was added. Nearly instantly, there should have been an emotional association; that's how the brain works. What was yours?" asked William.

"I thought it looked like pudding and baby poop," said Tom sheepishly.

William grinned but kept speaking. "OK, you had a couple of emotional associations put in the file based upon its visual appearance. One was negative and one was positive, but the negative one was stronger, at first, wasn't it?"

Tom grinned but said nothing. William continued.

"When I asked your *mind* to focus its intent on the thought of delicious brownies and hummus being right on top of them, you did, right?"

"Right," said Tom.

"Almost immediately the *brain* made a connection between brownies and hummus because of that intention, right?"

"Right again," said Tom.

"So your brain went from this," William said, pointing to the board.

I have no idea what hummus is.

"To this." He wrote on the board.

Hummus is like brownies.

"And we both know how you feel about baby poop and brownies. You see, Tom, the brain is a database of experiences and associations. It wants to make associations so that experiences can be filed appropriately. After your brain made the positive association between hummus and brownies, your mind told your brain's emotional association to be open to suggestion. The result was the action of eating the hummus." William turned to the board again and wrote.

I like hummus. Hummus is good.

"So the brain is this super computer that stores things and makes associations. When you open a file, there are related files—pictures, smells, and emotions—linked to it," offered Tom.

"Yes!" insisted William, eyes twinkling. "Go on."

"So ... the mind is the programmer that tells the brain which programs to run," said Tom, with a grin of dawning comprehension.

William waved his hands in the air to keep Tom talking.

"So my *mind* told my *brain* to hook how I feel about brownies to how I feel about hummus," said Tom with growing excitement.

"Yes! Yes! Yes! Tom, you are such a quick learner," said William, clapping his hands. "I swear that every kid should be taught a foreign language and mental programming before they enter high school!" exclaimed William. He walked over to Tom and gave him a one-armed hug. Mentally, William thanked one of his mentors, Dr. George DeSau.

William knelt down next to Tom so that they were at eye level. He stared at Tom for a second, as if to implant the next statement into his mind permanently.

"The important thing for your mind to remember is that your brain wants to build associations. As long as you are open to suggestion—or open to new possibilities—you can build new associations and delete old associations that have held you back in different areas of your life," said William.

William watched as his grandson tried to take all of this and internalize it. Tom had the look of someone who was daydreaming. William let him continue processing this new information until Tom looked at him directly. William walked back to the board and wrote.

As above, so below.

"One more association. There is an old saying: As above, so below. As you think, believe, and feel—in that lofty place above, where imagination, intention, and creativity circle in our dreams—that is where we build our reality. Over time, the things we have created fall like rain, and our physical reality blooms into existence," said William.

"If you want to throw in some science into this idea, there are subatomic particles that travel at the speed of light called neutrinos. As they slow down by entering a lower energetic state, they become part of the physical reality. Combine this with quantum entanglement. This spooky action at a distance is where two related particles are spinning in an observable direction. When separated and a force changes the spinning of the first particle, the second particle responds exactly the same even though there was no observable force. Since thoughts are energy, maybe they collide with neutrinos, cause them to change their spin and energetic state. You begin to construct your personal reality both 'here' and 'there.'"

Tom just stared at his grandpa with a stunned look and an open mouth.

"Sorry, Tom. That was too far down the rabbit hole for our first day. We'll just chalk that up to my own mental gymnastics. It's not like I'm going to give you a pop quiz on quantum mechanics."

"Grandpa, there is this kid in my class who always says he hates pop quizzes. He says they make him sick. As far as I know, he hasn't passed a pop quiz yet. Is that an example of 'As above, so below'?"

"Tom, that is a great example. It is also an example of something called NLP, or neurolinguistic programming."

Again, William walked to the board and wrote.

NLP—neurolinguistic programming

"We'll approach that momentarily," said William.
William erased what he had written on the board after making sure Tom had everything written down. He thought about asking Tom about the Latin phrase he had written earlier. Looking at the time, he decided against it and pressed onward by writing on the board.

Relaxation

"Relaxation is necessary for achieving alpha level, or lower, with your mind because your brain is a noisy thing. It is telling your body what to do, telling you how to act and respond in different situations, and filing and making associations with each experience that comes along. When the day is done, your brain is still processing all the data it received throughout the day. Even in dreams, your brain is working.

"However, if you remember the levels of activity of the brain, you will remember that beta is the working level. Your brain probably runs about fifteen to eighteen CPS because you are a young adult. As you get older and as you get involved in more and more complicated tasks, as you begin to do more than one task at a time—that's called multitasking—your brain will accelerate to twenty to twenty-two CPS, maybe even more.

"Controlled relaxation is a tool that your mind uses both to quiet itself and slow down the processing of the brain so that it slips into the alpha level. The alpha level is a very special place. That is where the mind can really get the attention of the brain. The two of them can work together more efficiently. It is where the reprogramming of old associations can happen. It is where new programs can be installed with a degree of confidence. The deeper you go into alpha, the better chance the programming has to remain. In fact, some people can even reprogram in theta, but that takes some practice. Can you think of some things that you would like to reprogram?"

Tom fidgeted in his seat as he thought about the past school year. He knew that his brother and most of his friends were going to be gone from school, but the thought of going back did not make him happy.

"I don't want to be afraid of going back to school," answered Tom.

"OK, let's work with that one. Tonight I will lead you through a controlled descent into the alpha level, and we'll reprogram that. Meanwhile, here's where we will pull NLP back into the discussion. For our purposes now, let us define NLP, which is also known as neurolinguistic programming. It is the study of words and the emotional content assigned to them. For example, if I say the word *brownie*, you have a positive response to that word, right?"

"You know it," smiled Tom.

"How about the word *Quan?*" asked William.

"Yeah, I like that word too," said Tom, smiling.

"How about the word *waddle?*" asked William.

The smile evaporated from Tom's face. His eyes had been shining brightly with the eagerness of learning. They now were dull and downcast as he remembered the humiliation he experienced in the school cafeteria. He went from thinking about the nickname Waddle to the nickname All-Scar. Tears were starting to well up in Tom's eyes.

William walked over to Tom and knelt beside him again. He hugged Tom and whispered an apology in his ear. William leaned back and lifted Tom's head with a finger under his chin.

"I'm sorry, Thomas. I did not know that word bothered you so much or I would have picked another example.

I did not want to hurt your feelings."

Tom wiped the fresh tears from his eyes and said, "Well, that's one example I will never forget."

"Let's wrap up this lesson for the day," said William. He wanted to change the environment or at least put some distance between himself and his faux pas.

"It's OK, Grandpa. We can keep going," said Tom.

"No, we need to spend some time with the trees," said William.

For a moment, William seemed to be disconnected from his body. He stood perfectly still, as though he were getting direction from outside of himself. Three seconds later, he abruptly sat down on the edge of his desk again.

"On second thought, think about your statement: 'I don't want to be afraid of going back to school.' Think how you can say the same thing in a positive manner. Think about the things that you say every day that could have a negative meaning. Chances are, you don't even know it. Rephrase it so that it is positive."

"So, that's my homework?"

"Well, coming up with a few negative phrases and rewriting them as positive is a start. Also, tell me who invented the light bulb in a report," replied William.

Tom stood up, chugged down his water, and followed his grandpa out to the garage. While his grandpa backed out the Jeep, Tom burped really loud and really long. Thinking he got away with something, he smiled brightly.

"Bodily sounds have emotional associations too?" asked William with a lopsided grin.

They looked at each other for a second before they both started to laugh. William pointed the Jeep into the woods where the trees were waiting for them. With the faux pas forgotten, Tom turned his face up to the sun and smiled. The Jeep ambled happily through the canopy of woods that created a kaleidoscope of sun and shadow. Moments later, Quan and Sid came bounding through the woods and escorted them to the excavation site.

Chapter 10 – Harvest

Just like the day before, both William and Tom labored in the sun and continued to dig a trench around the tree. The circle was completed by late afternoon. After a few minutes of rest, they started the same process on the second tree. Driving stakes and stringing twine to define the circle did not take long, so they got start on digging the second circle. A few hours later, mounds of dirt testified to the progress made before stopping for the day.

Back at the house, William prepared lunch while Tom showered. Tom took his time in the shower until the hot water made his skin lobster red. His tired and seldom-used muscles were aching from the long hours and physical labor in the sun of the past two days. Judging from their progress to date, it shouldn't take too much longer to get a perimeter dug around the trees. William had told him that there was a machine that could uproot both tree and root cluster and drive it to its new home, so the hardest part would be done by machine.

Tom was pleasantly surprised by Grandpa's choice of lunch—homemade pizza. Other than cheese and mushrooms, it was covered by the various herbs William had grown in his garden. Tom usually liked pepperoni and pineapple on his pizza, but this one was good—it was both tasty and familiar looking. William teased him by saying that dinner would be salad, baba ganoush, and tabouli. Tom wasn't sure if he was kidding or not. After lunch was over, William directed Tom back to the basement to do more research. Tom made his way back to the library, and William pulled some food out of the freezer for dinner and went about his chores around the house.

William went out to the patio and watered and trimmed the herbs and plants that he grew for both cooking and medicinal purposes. He dabbled in several fields of interest. One of them was called naturopathic healing. One component, nutrition, was his favorite. He grew several different kinds of plants and used them for various ailments. Feverfew, chamomile, nightshade, and mint were just a few of the plants he grew. He used to use a mortar and pestle to grind up his dried plants, but recently, he had started using a small food processor, as more and more of his neighbors began to request his ointments for muscle pain and his teas for people who had trouble sleeping. Currently, he was working on a deal to have a small display in the town's local specialty store. If that worked out, he was thinking of even making homemade herbal soap to complete his line of products.

Once he fed the plants, he went to his office in the barn and called his factory. He was retired in the sense that he did not go into work every day. However, he did talk to the office manager once a week to see how things were going and if any special design requests had come in. Although he had the staff to handle such things, he liked to see what designs people came up with so that his mind stayed fresh and current on decorating trends. Sometimes the in-store designer would e-mail him custom designs and ask him for input.

After he chatted with the folks at the office, William pulled out a file from his desk. It was almost as thick as a telephone book. Inside this file were all the documents he had ever created, referenced, or received while he worked as a personal coach/instructor. He had taught aspects of human performance improvement, as a class, for several years. About ten years ago, though, he put all his energy into getting his cabin finished, getting his carpentry business on the Internet, and getting people comfortable in their positions so that he could spend less time there and more time pursuing his hobbies. It seemed to him that the Universe was telling him to get back to teaching human development. First his neighbor had some problems where memory pegs helped. Now, his grandson needed more generalized help. William decided to refresh himself in the scientific research that provided the credible foundation to his teaching.

By the time dinner was a concern, William had wrapped up what he was doing and headed back to the house. He lit the charcoal in the grill on the patio and then went into the kitchen, where thawed salmon filets were waiting. After a dash of seasoning, William put them on the highest rack of the grill and then added a handful of wood from an apple tree to the coals. He also put more of the wood in a small metal container, sprayed a bit of water on the wood, and then set it in with the salmon. Later, once the fire cooled a bit, he put two ears of corn onto the grill. While the fish and corn cooked, William put together a salad to go with dinner. He was adding the finishing touches to the salad when Tom came upstairs.

"So, you're done with your research just in time for dinner?" asked William.

"Well, I was able to find out a lot of details, but I have just started writing. I thought I would come up and see what was really for dinner," said Tom.

"Smoked salmon, grilled corn on the cob, and a salad is what's really for dinner," said William with a grin.

"It smells great. Maybe I can get the report written before I go to bed tonight," said Tom thoughtfully.

"Actually, I think it would make interesting dinner conversation. Why don't you just tell me what you have discovered?" said William.

Relieved he did not have to write, Tom gave him a nod and went back downstairs. A few moments later, he returned with his notes. Once he was seated comfortably in the kitchen, he began.

"OK, well, the first thing is that most people believe that Thomas Edison was the inventor of the light bulb. But he wasn't the only one. Both Edison and another guy, Sir Joseph Wilson Swan of England, invented it in eighteen seventy-nine. And they really didn't even invent it. They were just improving on a design that was already out there," said Tom.

William set the table and encouraged Tom to continue while he wrapped things up in the kitchen.

"So, how do you feel about that?" asked William.

"Well, guys in my school would call them posers."

William looked at Tom with an inquisitive furrowed brow.

"Posers are people who act like they know something but they really don't. They try to act cool about stuff they have never tried ... they're imposters," answered Tom.

Tom referred to his notes and then continued. "Anyway, the whole electric bulb idea actually started with a guy named Sir Humphrey Davy. In eighteen eleven, he discovered that an electrical arc jumped between two poles and made light. These electric arc lights were actually on display in eighteen forty-one as public lighting along the Place de la Concorde in Paris."

"Hmm ... the city of lights," said William. "Remind you of our experiment yesterday?"

"Yeah, it sure did," answered Tom.

"The problem with the arc light was that they burned out too quickly, and another way of doing it was needed. The guy who found another way of doing it was James P. Joule. He determined that if the arc were replaced with a piece of material between the poles, heat energy in the material would become light energy."

William brought the food to the table, and the discussion was temporarily halted while they had dinner. The table wasn't completely silent. Different grunts and groans indicating how much they enjoyed the dinner were occasionally exchanged. When dinner was nearly over, William asked Tom to continue with his story.

"This Joule guy is so famous that they named a measurement after him. Somewhere I read that they measure electricity in Joules."

"Yes, and someday when you take physics you will learn more about Joule. You'll also hear about Mach, Watt, and others," said William. "Tell me more about the light bulb."

"Well, Edison had this team of people working for him. They were called the Edison Pioneers. They were taking everything they could imagine to make these pieces of material give off light. They called this piece of the light bulb the filament. One of the ways they tried to solve the problem of the burning filament was to get rid of the oxygen in the bulb.

"The problem was that oxygen was like food for the fire. They needed to design a light bulb that would not have any oxygen in it so that the filament wouldn't have any food. Then the filament would take longer to wear out.

"Then in January eighteen seventy-nine, Edison and his Pioneers had built his first electric light. It worked by sending electricity through a thin filament made of platinum. It was built inside a glass vacuum bulb. It worked for a little while, but after a couple of hours, it burned out too."

By this time, William had cleared the table. He grabbed his jacket and sat down to hear the rest of the story. It was getting close to the time Sid and Quan would be awaiting their dinner.

"Here's where it gets interesting, Grandpa. The one book I was reading said that two of the Edison Pioneers, Lewis Latimer and Joseph V. Nichols, received the patent for their invention of the first light bulb with a carbon filament and not Edison. The light bulb with the carbon filament glowed continuously for forty hours.

"But, another book I read said that Edison was sitting around one day and just imagined that a string, which was carbonized, would be the solution. That book does not even mention the Latimer guy or the Nichols guy."

"So, why do you think that those two gentlemen were left out of the other book?" asked William.

"I think that either the person writing the book did not do their homework or they were prejudiced against them," said Tom.

"Why do you say that?" asked William.

"Because I looked up the Latimer guy. He was a real genius. He taught himself to be a scientist. He was a technical artist who worked for Alexander Graham Bell before he worked for Edison. Latimer also has the patent for the carbon filament. Someone who is that smart should be as famous as Edison. Instead, no one has even heard of him. It seems pretty fishy to me."

"Tom, me thinkest something smellest rotten in Denmark," said William, who knew he was going to get a peculiar look from Tom. Tom did not disappoint him.

"The thing is," Tom continued, "Latimer was the only black member of Edison's Pioneers. I think he got ignored because he was black."

William thought for a second and then said, "Tom, the world is full of injustices and half-truths. Some are comfortable living with the lie. Some are not, and they work to change it. Then there are the masses who don't even know they are living with the lie. They are not curious enough to think for themselves but would rather someone else tell them how to live and what to believe. If it weren't for the people who question the answers, we would still be living on a flat earth comprised mostly of land. Someday, I want to read you something called the 'Crazy Ones'. It is homage to the poet Jack Kerouac."

With dinner over, they both walked downstairs and out to the garage where an impatient Sid and a playful Quan were waiting. Together, they prepared bowls for the dogs to eat. Tom watched how William fixed Sid's bowl and then he did the same with Quan's. Before they set down their bowls, they went through the sternum tapping of the thymus gland that they had done earlier. Tom still thought it was a bit odd, but the dogs didn't seem to mind. In fact, it looked as though they enjoyed it, so Tom tapped away.

Once the dogs were eating, William and Tom took their walk down the pathway to the road. The sun was no longer visible, but the muted colors in the sky were starting to fade, just as hot iron does as it cools. William decided to bring up the subject of neurolinguistic programming again.

"So have you thought of a positive way to say what you did in class today?" asked William.

"How about this: I am not afraid to go back to school. Does that work?" asked Tom.

"Well, it is an improvement. I was thinking of removing all negative words like *afraid* from the statement.

Want to try again?" asked William.

"I will be happy to go back to school. Better?" inquired Tom.

"Yes, that is better. Now think about this. Your sentence is in the future tense because you used the word *will*. Try present tense," advised William.

"OK, I am happy to go back to school," stated Tom.

"That's it. Take the negative and make it a positive. Then, make sure there is also a positive emotion attached to that comment. Words are important, but your intent is more so," said William.

"So, what would have to happen at school for you to love going? What kind of change do you want to create to make it something you love?" asked William.

Without much hesitation, Tom responded, "I'd like to have a girlfriend."

"A girlfriend? Already? Why do you want a girlfriend at this age?" asked William with arched eyebrows.

"I don't want that kind of girlfriend, Grandpa. I mean, I want a friend who just happens to be a girl."

"Just happens to be a girl, huh?" asked William with a mischievous grin.

"I want to know what girls think about and why they chose the boyfriends that they do. I liked this one girl in my class, but I had no idea what to say to her except hi ... and that doesn't get you too far."

"No, it doesn't. But, it is something we can work on during your relaxation session later. Oh, and by the way, every guy in the world sometimes wonders what girls are thinking. So don't feel like you're the first to think of it," said William in a reassuring tone.

"OK," said Tom.

Chapter 11 – Asleep and Awake

On their way back from the road, Sid and Quan caught up to them and, as usual, escorted them back to the house. Once they were at the steps leading up to the deck, the dogs took off in the direction of the barn to see if there was anything worth chasing. William and Tom ambled up the steps and into the house. While Tom cleaned up his research in the basement, William lit a small fire in the fireplace. He then put on some music, a soothing duet between a classical guitar and a cello. William let out an audible sigh of contentment.

"Ah, Andrés Segovia," whispered William.

After they both got ready for bed, William met Tom in the main room, where the fire and the music were still having a muted conversation. William had Tom sit in a chair and get comfortable.

"OK, I am going to have you close your eyes, relax, and pretend that you are alone in a movie theater. I will tell you a story and you will imagine that it is a movie playing on the screen. Now, feel your eyelids getting heavy. As you close your eyes, feel yourself becoming more relaxed. As I count from ten down to one, you will become more and more relaxed. Take nice deep breaths from your belly. That's good. Here we go," said William.

As William counted down, Tom closed his eyes and felt himself drifting almost immediately. He found himself in that place, just before you go to sleep, where you can still hear what is going on around you but, occasionally, a fragment of a dream will creep into your thoughts.

He heard his grandpa counting, but he also saw Quan chasing her tail while he and Little Eagle watched and laughed.

William counted down to five and then counted slower and slower until he got to one.

He stopped speaking for a moment to listen to Tom breathe. He was not too sure if he was asleep or if he was just really relaxed. He decided to continue with the alpha programming.

"Tom, I want you to imagine that you are in a movie theater all by yourself. Can you imagine that?" asked William.

Tom was silent for a few seconds. He seemed to be asleep. Just as William was going to ask him again, Tom made a groan that sounded in the affirmative.

"Tom, I want you to imagine that the comfortable chair you are in now is the chair that is in the middle of the movie theater. You are very comfortable and cozy in the theater. Now, look up at the screen. See the curtains pull back completely to expose the entire screen. See the screen turn from black to gray. Can you see this?" asked William.

"Yeah," slurred Tom.

"The movie is about to start. You can hear the projector running softly in the background. There is soft music playing. Gradually, the picture brightens. It is sunrise. You are standing in front of a building that seems familiar. As the sky brightens, you are able to see the front of your school. It is still early and no one is around. Tell me what the yard looks like," asked William.

With a sleepy mumble, Tom replied, "I see trees and bushes. I see a flagpole. I see bricks and windows."

"I want you to look closely at the closest tree. I want you to feel it and tell me what it feels like."

Tom muttered, "It feels kind of rough and smooth. It has a tingle to it, like electricity."

"Tom, when I asked you to go to the tree, did you walk over to it or did you just imagine being next to it?"

"I wanted to be next to it, so I was."

"Tom, in physics, all things have a vibrational rate. The atoms and molecules that make up a thing have energy. Look at the tree and tell me if you notice anything special or unique."

"Yeah, I can see a vapor coming off of it. It seems like there is a vapor about an inch around it."

"That's good, Tom. Do you see the same thing around the bushes?"

"Yes. They have it too."

"Tom, touch the building and tell me what you feel."

"It kind of feels like electricity too. It's barely there, but it is. It's more like an itch than a tingle."

"Step back from the school and sit back in the chair. See the school from its original distance. This time see the trees and bushes with a vapor around them. Know that they are vibrating. See the building. Know that it vibrates. When you look at the picture now, what do you see?"

108

"It looks like it has been painted with brighter colors than before," said Tom.

"When you look at the school, are you excited or interested in being around that energy? When we go out into the trees, do you like being around that energy? When you are in the library, do you like being around that energy?"

"Yes, I do," answered Tom.

"Then realize that you are always surrounded by this energy. It is in all things.

When you look at the picture of the school now, how does it make you feel?"

"It makes me curious."

"Good, curiosity is a wonderful thing. Keep that with you wherever you go. You will uncover secrets and mysteries wherever you apply your curiosity. People will find you interesting because you use your curiosity in such a unique way. People will admire you. When you return to school, full of the energy that people and things bring to your surroundings, people will see you differently. They will want you to be their friend. Now, how do you feel about going back to school?" asked William.

"I feel pretty stoked about it," said Tom.

William flashed his signature lopsided grin, "Does stoked mean happy?"

"Yes," said Tom.

"Then let me hear you say that you are happy at school," said William.

"I am happy when I am at school," said Tom.

William continued to have Tom make associations in his mind by comparing school to brownies, hummus, the woods, Quan, and other things with positive emotional content. To make school more desirable, William added another component. He told Tom that he would meet his girlfriend there too.

"Tom, when you are in the alpha level, you will have more self-confidence, you will have improved health, you will be able to reprogram your mind with greater ease, and the new associations will be much stronger than the old ones you have replaced. In fact, deleted associations will remain deleted. Whenever you reprogram your brain's associations, they must be for the greater good for you and your circle of influence. You can never reprogram your brain for negative associations. Your mind will never allow associations that are bad or hurtful to yourself or others. Do you understand?" asked William.

"Tom, do you understand?"

Finally, Tom answered, "Yeah."

"Tom, when you want to achieve the alpha level in the future, you will be able to do so by counting down from ten to one slowly. You will also be able to do this by closing your eyes and touching the tip of your index finger to the tip of your thumb. This action will act as a switch enabling you to achieve the alpha level for any positive purpose you desire. If you wish it and it is for a greater good, then it will be so. Do you understand?" asked William.

"Yes," said Tom.

"Now, I want you to get up and walk to your bedroom. Know where all obstacles are in the room and avoid them. Once you are in your bedroom, get into bed and await further direction."

While William was speaking, he took a book off the coffee table and placed it directly in Tom's path to his room. As Tom stood up, William remained directly behind him so that he could catch him if he should fall, though William was fairly certain that he would not. Tom stood up, walked to the book, stepped over the book, and then went to his room where he pulled back the covers and laid down. During the whole trip, Tom's eyes never opened. William brought a chair over and sat it at the foot of Tom's bed. He had a couple more programming things he wanted to get into his head.

"Tom, the difference between a genius and a regular person is that the genius uses their brain differently. You are a genius because you are now using your brain differently.

"Tom, the difference between alchemists and normal people is that alchemists question what is and they recognize the energy in all things and respect it. They are always willing to question their own beliefs—scientific or spiritual. You are an alchemist because you question what is. As evidence, I remind you of your research on Columbus and Edison. You recognize the energy in all things and respect it. As evidence, I remind you of your own observation of the trees, bushes, and brick building. You are willing to question your own beliefs. As evidence, I remind you of your enthusiasm upon discovering Quan and Sid in the woods."

"Tom, you will recognize the negative words in your vocabulary such as *can't, hate, makes me sick,* a *pain in the neck,* and other similar words. Words are sound. Sound is vibration. Vibration is energy. Avoid negative energy, and, instead, use words and phrases in a positive fashion.

"Tom, continue to relax and have a peaceful sleep. When you awaken tomorrow, you will be refreshed and relaxed, and your muscles will be completely rejuvenated. You will meet the day with enthusiasm and natural curiosity. Sleep well and remember that Grandpa loves you."

William picked the chair up off the floor and set it quietly under the desk. He closed the door to the bedroom and circled into his own bedroom. He decided that he, too, should do some meditation at alpha level before going to bed. He went out to the kitchen, grabbed a glass of cold water, and headed back to his room. On his way, he stubbed his toe on a book lying on the floor. Snorting with amusement, William returned the book to the coffee table, went to his bedroom, and slid beneath the covers on his bed. Gentle wisps of fire were running out of wood to burn as he closed his eyes. Soon, William's programming became a peaceful sleep as well.

Chapter 12 – Surprises

Early morning mist blanketed the quiet forest and was slow to surrender to the morning sun. Sitting on a fallen moss-covered log alongside the creek on William's property, Little Eagle watched a family of deer drink their fill. The father of this family stood guard while the rest of the family had their share.

"Go ahead, Brother Deer, I will make sure no harm comes to you."

The big buck obliged and drank deeply as well. As they wandered back into the woods, a new sound came to Little Eagle's attention.

"I wondered how soon you would come back to see me. Are you learning many things?"

Out from a cluster of bushes by the water's edge, Tom stepped onto the bank of the creek.

"I have been learning a lot of things. Really cool stuff too. The funny thing is that it seems that when you have an answer, it is still a question," answered Tom.

"Yes, many things are not as they appear. Sometimes this is good, sometimes it's bad."

A ray of sunshine appeared on the rock next to Little Eagle. He climbed off of the log and positioned himself under the light. He laid back on the rock and sighed contentedly. Tom picked his way across the stream, trying not to get his shoes wet.

"If you don't want to get your shoes wet, just be here," said Little Eagle.

"Be here?" asked Tom.

"Yes. Just like you did with the tree in front of the school. Just think and be."

Tom closed his eyes and thought about sitting on the log where Little Eagle had been.

"Much better," said Little Eagle.

"Holy cow!" shouted Tom. Little Eagle's voice was immediately next to him. He opened his eyes and found himself on the log exactly where he imagined.

"How did I do that?" asked Tom.

"Think about it. You are the genius. You are the alchemist's heir. You tell me how you did it," instructed Little Eagle.

"Oh, I'm dreaming," surmised Tom. Little Eagle smiled.

"Are you a wizard too?" asked Tom.

"No. I think the best way to describe me is somewhere between a guide and a map," said Little Eagle.

"Are you going to take me somewhere?"

"No place that you don't want to go. I just want to make sure that you don't get lost or confused. Instead of discovering things in the woods by stomping around in circles and scaring off anything that's not deaf, I want to show you how to follow a path quietly and completely. I want to show you how to take in everything that you see without trying to possess it. After all, the adventure lays in the trip itself and not the destination," replied Little Eagle.

"Are you going to help me like going to school too?" asked Tom.

"No, I am going to help you like yourself. Someday you will leave school, but you will always have to live with yourself," said Little Eagle.

"Good point. So how are you going to do that?" asked Tom.

"A person is measured not only by what they say but also by what they do. I am going to give you an opportunity to learn about self-reliance. I will be with you at all times, although you may not know it. As you pass through a challenge, the world of possibilities will be much broader than you currently understand it."

Without fear or worry, Tom responded, "OK. What should I do in the meantime?"

"Don't push the river ... just relax" said Little Eagle.

At the same time, William was dreaming. He was in a clearing in the woods and was sitting at a campfire. He was much younger than he was now. He looked to be about sixteen years old. Although the body was much younger, William still had the same sagacious eyes and lopsided smile. He was speaking to a very old American Indian who was sitting next to him.

This was no ordinary Indian. He was from a powerful line of shaman; many would say he inherited the same gift of vision his great-grandfather had. Songs and stories were still told of his gift of vision.

115

The light from the campfire illuminated many different wrinkles and scars on his face, illustrating the years of pain and wisdom that he carried. In his weathered hands, he held a hand-carved pipe with two feathers attached to it.

"Grandfather, I have worked hard to pass on the ways of the ancestors. However, I have found that most people are not interested in those ways," said William. "In many ways, times have changed and the people have changed with it."

The Indian took the pipe in his mouth and then removed a stick from the fire. He lit the pipe with great satisfaction and a certain degree of ceremony. Once the pipe was fully lit, he closed his eyes and pulled on it a few times so that the smoke would surround them both. While his eyes were still closed, he sighed in deep contentment. Finally, he looked at the younger William.

"Have patience, little one, and do not fear change. The one you teach now is the vanguard of greater changes to come, just as the Indigo children made a path for the Crystal children. Many will recognize these are good changes. However, some will keep their eyes closed and will not see. He will lead the way as certain and inevitable as a new dawn creeps over the hills. Even now, he prepares to accept his life's mission," answered the ancient Indian.

"Thank you, Grandfather, for sharing this with me. I see that he has a curiosity about his reality that 'civilized' society has not crushed into apathy or conformity. I am encouraging his curiosity and

116

appreciation of Mother Earth. What else can I do to help him along this path?" asked William.

The Indian drew again on the pipe. He appeared to be recalling something that was stored way back in his memory. Eventually, he smiled, having found what he wanted to say. He gave a small pull on the pipe for emphasis and then spoke.

"Little one, I acknowledge your efforts and intent and see that it is good. I think that this should continue. You are correct in recognizing his awakening to the elements around him. To recognize that one's words as well as deeds can direct energy is also wise. I look forward and see that his self-reliance is important too. If wisdom is water, self-reliance is the vessel that holds it."

"Thank you, Grandfather. I will give him opportunity to help himself," answered William.

"Let us sit a while and enjoy," said the Indian, who pointed to the fire with one hand and extended the pipe to William with the other.

Together they sat watching the ballet of fire. They passed the pipe back and forth and thought of the times that had been and the times yet to pass. It was a moment outside of time where student and teacher enjoyed the simple pleasure of each other's company. When it came time for parting, the Indian had one more piece of advice for young William.

"Relax ... and try not to push the river."

The next morning, Tom was up with the sun and first into the kitchen. He looked around for coffee. He wanted to make some for his grandpa, but was unable to find it. He also realized that he didn't know what Grandpa ate for breakfast either. With such a handicap, he decided to hop in the shower and then get dressed. He was almost finished with the shower when he realized that his muscles hardly ached at all. It was as if he had not been working at ditch digging for the past couple of days, but had just slept in an awkward position. By the time he was dressed and on his way out to the kitchen, he had no aches or pains at all.

As he meandered out to the kitchen, he smelled the distinctive aroma of brewing coffee. William was dressed in a dark sports coat and khaki pants. He had his tie flipped up over his left shoulder as his sipped coffee from one hand and read paperwork with the other. Apparently, this day was going to be as unusual as the day before. His grandpa, yet again, had surprised him at breakfast.

"Good morning, Tom. Did you sleep well?"

"Yeah, I did. It's amazing because when I woke up this morning I was not tired or exhausted.

In fact, I was in the shower when I realized that my muscles weren't sore ... they felt pretty good," said Tom.

"Good, I'm glad. What about last night's programming session? What did you think about that?" asked William.

"Well, it was comfortable and weird at the same time. I think I was both asleep and awake. Kind of like a balloon, I would start to float away and then you would talk and it would pull me back down," said Tom.

William smiled and nodded in complete understanding.

"Why are you all dressed up today, Grandpa?" asked Tom.

"Well, there is a client who wants to meet me before they send a bunch of business my way. If everything goes well, we will be making custom cabinetry for an architect who constructs some very nice homes. In return, his crew will volunteer a few hours for Habitat for Humanity. So, I need to go into work for probably the entire day. I will be back before sunset though."

"What should I do?" asked Tom.

"I want you to go about your day as if I was here. I want you to do some digging—both literally and literary. Once you get back from the woods, I want you to tell me who invented the radio," said William.

"OK. Based upon what I've done so far I'm guessing that the inventor is not *the* inventor," said Tom.

"Would I be correct in assuming that you have had driver's training?" asked William.

The abrupt change in discussion topics was a mental speed bump for Tom. It took him a couple of seconds to replay what his grandpa had said. Sensing something exciting about to happen, Tom's heart beat a little faster.

"Actually, I was going to be doing that this summer. But I have been driving the pickup truck around the farm when Dad needs a hand repairing something," said Tom slowly. He was trying to see where the discussion was going.

"All right then, I want you to drive the Jeep to the road and back. I will meet you outside when you get back," said William.

William grabbed a small ring of keys from the counter and flipped them to Tom. Tom caught them, quickly finished putting on his sneakers, and ran out to the Jeep in front of the garage. He hopped behind the wheel and almost started it up. Finally, his excitement abated long enough for his training to come to the forefront of his mind. He remembered what his Dad had taught him.

He looked at all the mirrors to see that they were positioned correctly for him. He put on his seat belt and then looked around his surroundings to make sure no obstacles were near the vehicle. With all the prestart checks completed, he put the key in the ignition and turned the key to adult emancipation. The engine surged to life and was ready to go. Tom remembered to give his surroundings a quick look and put the car in gear. With a grin so wide it hurt his cheeks, he put his foot on the gas pedal.

The Jeep lurched as if it wanted to go but it didn't. Tom gave it more gas and again it lurched with a whining noise. Tom stopped and put the vehicle back into park, looked over the gauges, and finally saw the problem. A small red light illuminated the word *brake*. A flush of embarrassment made the tips of his ears match the red dash light. He released the parking break lever located between the seats. Once again, Tom repeated his sequence and finally started to move. He moved slowly, with a deliberate pace, as if to examine every inch of ground he was about to roll over. He finally settled down and made the

120

half-mile drive to the main road. No traffic was coming from either direction, so Tom drove out onto the roadway and turned around. His trip back to the house was confident and brisk. He pulled up to the garage where William was waiting.

"Fine job, my boy. You now have stewardship of the place until I return. I have my cell phone with me, so I will call you to let you know when I am on my way home," said William, walking up to the Jeep.

"Why did you have me drive out to the road and back, Grandpa?" asked Tom as he turned off the ignition.

"Because you will be using the Jeep to get back to the trees. Just go about your day as if I were with you. I have other transportation."

With that, William headed into the barn. Tom stood there for a second—Grandpa must have another car hidden somewhere. Tom discovered he was becoming used to being surprised. In fact, he almost expected his grandpa to appear in a rocket-propelled car that had been hidden in a cave. Tom chuckled aloud. If his grandpa came out wearing a cape, he was going to faint. As it just so happened, it was even more surprising than that.

When a rough staccato sound came from the barn, Tom started walking toward the open barn door. A deep, grumbling roar emanated from the barn. Just as he thought what it was, it rumbled out the door. William had an old-fashioned helmet and aviator goggles on his head. He was wearing a full-length leather coat like cowboys wore.

Underneath him, a restored but very old motorcycle with an Indian head mounted on the front wheel fender growled with potential.

William smiled and revved the engine, and the noise graduated to an organized roar. He put the beast into gear with his left hand and rolled away from Tom toward the roadway. Tom stood there for a good twenty seconds with his mouth wide open before he realized it. He closed his mouth, shaking his head in disbelief. He walked over to the barn door, closed it, and headed back into the house, still reeling with the thought in his head: Who *was* William Miller?

Chapter 13 – Self-reliance

Tom sat at the kitchen table eating the last of the muffins and drinking a glass of apple juice. As he stared at the kitchen table top, he wondered who this man was. First and foremost, this man was Grandpa. Grandpa was the kindly gentleman who came to visit occasionally, came to all the family functions, and was always ready to listen to you.

He was so much more, though. He was a carpenter, a businessman, a salesman, an artist, a scientist, a teacher, a husband, a father, and who knows what else? Tom also realized, though, that he was not just what he did. Tom went to school and built models, but there was more to him than that. What did Grandpa believe? Who were his idols? These were all things that he wanted to find out. However, today was not that day, since his grandpa was wheeling down a highway somewhere.

The day was getting along, so Tom thought that he should too. He filled up a plastic pitcher with ice water and headed out to the Jeep. More confident now than earlier this morning, Tom got into the Jeep and started it without any problem. The drive out to the work site was exciting for Tom; he was both driving and on his own. He took no notice that the sun was not shining through the trees because the skies were overcast. Of course, Quan was showing him the way.

Tom worked hard with both shovel and pick. The Jeep's radio kept him company as Quan was elsewhere. He was determined to make decent headway to please his grandpa, and, since his muscles were not hurting, he thought it was the perfect opportunity to make some extra progress. It was a humid and overcast day as Tom toiled under the second tree. It wasn't until late afternoon that he took a break and noticed the ominous sky. He really wanted to make a good impression with the trench, so he decided to keep working until it started to rain. At that point, he could still put the tools under the tarp, hop in the Jeep, and head back without getting too wet. He took a water break and listened to the radio in the Jeep to see if the bad weather was heading his way or if it was just passing nearby.

When no news indicated that he should do otherwise, he turned off the radio and went back to work. About twenty minutes later, the rain started to fall, so Tom stored the tools under the tarp and got into the Jeep. He turned the key in the ignition but nothing happened. Apparently the battery was old or not keeping a charge. So with the rain growing steadily harder, Tom sat in the Jeep with a dead battery and wondered what to do next.

The rumble of thunder did nothing to help Tom with his attempts to concentrate. He knew that, eventually, Grandpa would come home and see that the Jeep was missing. He would, more than likely, come out and find him sitting here looking pitiful. At the same time, he did not know how late Grandpa would be getting back home. He said he would call him about dinner time. That meant that he'd be home later than that. Tom needed to get back to the house by dinner time to feed the dogs too. Rain kept pelting the soft top of the Jeep, harder for a while and then softer. The time between the thunder and the lightning was decreasing. His dad had taught him that meant that the storm was coming closer. Finally, he decided to leave the Jeep and walk back to the house. He could feed the dogs, get clean, warm, and dry, and wait for his grandpa's phone call.

When Tom got out of the Jeep, it was starting to rain hard again. At the last second, Tom decided to take the tarp off the tools and cover himself with it as best he could. He needed the cover more than the tools did. He started jogging down the trail toward the house. Although he was immediately soaked, Tom was determined to get back to the house. Soon, the rain intensified—so much so that the raindrops felt like stinging bees. When he saw the bouncing white pebbles on the ground, he realized that there was pea-sized hail coming down too. Pulling his arms under the tarp for some protection, Tom left the trail and ran for the cover of the darkening woods.

Once he was into the woods, the canopy of trees was able to protect him somewhat, but the wind and hail were still strong enough to pelt him every so often. Occasionally, a flash of lightning or a crack of thunder would seem to appear directly above him and would startle him greatly. The panic in his chest made him feel as though his heart wanted burst. He felt short of breath and was nearly on the verge of tears. If he had known that he was in the middle of a severe thunderstorm and that a tornado was forming less than a mile away, he would have been frightened to the point of hysterics.

When he arrived at the creek, he was shocked to see that it was much wider now—maybe twice as deep as before and moving much faster. Tom knew from watching TV shows that people could be swept away by currents if they were not careful. Watching all the branches and other flotsam go by, he decided to walk along the stream and see if there was a shallow or narrow place to cross. It sounded like a good plan, but there was no path. He had to pick his way through the weeds and tree roots while making sure that he did not slip and fall into the rushing waters.

For almost half an hour, Tom carefully picked his way along the riparian edge and paid particular attention to where he walked. The hail had stopped torturing him and the wind had died down, so it was easier. It was then he noticed the sky had an ominous green tint to it. From a video he had watched online, he knew that the possibility of a tornado existed. He looked up occasionally to see if the skies would tell him anything more, but the trees obstructed his view of the sky almost entirely. Finally, he saw something that looked promising—a fallen tree.

At the water's edge, a tree's root system had been eroding for some time, and then it had fallen under its own weight. Based upon the moss and rot on parts of the log, Tom thought that it had probably been there for years. Looking at the distance between where the tree met the swollen creek and where the opposite bank was, Tom felt that he could jump most of the distance. It really didn't matter if his shoes got wet at this point. He snorted a soggy laugh and decided to go for it.

He carefully examined the log and looked for potential hazards. Tom took a deep breath, summoned up his courage, and climbed up the cluster of roots and onto the log. Very carefully, he walked down the log as if it were a tightrope. Finally, he was standing about four feet from where the tree met the water's edge. Suddenly, Tom had an image in his mind of his brother. He had been at a track meet with his family to see Mark compete. He remembered Mark doing a standing broad jump. The imagery held no emotional content; Tom saw it as an opportunity to save himself. He looked at the bank, visualized the body mechanics involved, took a deep breath, and made his leap.

Several unexpected things happened simultaneously. Tom's last step was on a mossy spot that had no traction, so Tom did not get the push-off he had hoped for. He also did not expect the rotted wood under water to break off as he was jumping from it. Having no support or forward momentum, Tom crashed into the rushing water. The water was only about hip deep, but being off balance, Tom was completely submerged for a second.

He fought to stand up, but the current was too strong. Tom was pulled into the stream. Frantically, he grasped at anything he could find. Many of the pieces of broken tree limbs were no bigger than a broom handle. He finally got his feet under him and tried again to stand up. Again, he failed, except this time he swallowed a mouthful of the mucky, turbulent water. Gasping and choking, Tom grabbed at a cluster of exposed roots passing by his head. He got it!

Tom's legs were quickly swept out from under him and the force of the current bore down on him as he hung on with one hand. He reached up twice trying to find a hold for his other hand. He couldn't find one. The muscles in Tom's arm burned from the exertion, and he knew he would soon lose his grip.

The thought of drowning gave him the burst of energy he needed. He got a leg under him, pushed up, and grabbed another root with the other hand. He pulled himself slowly out of the water. Finally, Tom was completely out of the water and draped across the exposed roots of an old, gnarled tree. Tom had never seen anything so beautiful in his life.

The rain fell harder again a few minutes later. Tom wanted to get away from the growing creek, so he crawled to the top of the embankment and laid against a tree for a moment or two. He started shivering and pulled the tarp tighter around him. Was he going into shock? He decided that, whatever it was, he needed to conserve body heat. He took the leaves that surrounded him and stuffed them into his shirt and pants, thinking that they would create a barrier between him and his wet clothes as well as act as insulation. Exhausted from his efforts and having no idea where he was, Tom curled up under a pine tree and rested.

His rest did not last long, as the rest of his body decided to report in like wounded soldiers. Of course, the muscles of his right arm were very sore from hanging on for dear life. His back and shoulders were sore from the work earlier that day. He noticed that his left ankle was throbbing but could not remember twisting it. Maybe when he was being buffeted in the creek, he had twisted it while trying to stand. The mouthful of muddy creek water he had swallowed did not make him feel well either. Feeling a little warmer and quite confident that resting further was out of the question, he rolled out from his cover and started back toward the creek. This lasted about two steps.

Tom's ankle was just not going to cooperate. Tom hobbled to another tree and leaned against it as though he was drawing strength from it. Finally, all that he had been through in the past couple of hours overwhelmed him. Tears swam with raindrops as he tilted his face toward the heavens and shouted.

"Why!?"

Tom hobbled back to his cover under the boughs of the pine tree and cried softly. He was nowhere near the Jeep. He knew Grandpa could not ride in the rain and he would be late. He could not walk without a great deal of pain, and darkness would be upon him soon. Following the creek back to the path would have been impossible. While weighing his options and for some reason he could not justify, he started singing a song that was one of his mom's favorites ... something about raindrops falling on his head. When he got to a part where he forgot the words, he stopped and looked around. If he was going to find a walking stick, he needed the rest of what remaining light there was to find it. As he scanned the ground closest to him, he realized that he was not alone. Something was moving in the woods ... and whatever it was, it was big.

Tom's heart was thumping so hard in his chest that it drowned out the sound of the wind, rain, and angry creek. Tom imagined all sorts of animals that might be in the woods. All of them would consider him a tasty dinner. Waves of nausea joined the pounding in his chest as he widened his eyes to see what beast had come for him. Suddenly, a loud, sharp bark creased the air. Tom immediately knew to whom that bark belonged.

"Quan!" shouted Tom.

Immediately, a thrashing of underbrush was heard to his left. A furry black and tan blur bounded through the tall grass, which parted like the wake of a boat. Quan came bounding up to him and then danced in a circle and barked, as if to celebrate finding him.

"Quan, I am so glad to see you!" exclaimed Tom through both tears and a smile.

He grabbed her and scrubbed her head and ears. Quan licked his face and then collapsed at his side. She rolled over and waited for Tom to scratch her belly. He was more than happy to oblige. He laid his head on Quan's side and patted her lovingly. Suddenly, she jumped up and took a few steps away from Tom. She looked back and waited for him. He stood up and looked at the ground intensely. Within a few painful steps, Tom found a thin, short piece of wood that would serve as a walking stick. He leaned on it a few times to see if it would bear his weight. Once satisfied, he looked at Quan.

"Quan, get me out of here."

Quan gave her tail a wag and into the woods she went. Tom did his best to follow after her. It wasn't too long before Quan realized that Tom was moving too slow, so she came back closer to him—so close that it seemed that she was on an invisible leash. As they walked, Tom found a better piece of wood to serve as a walking stick; their pace quickened a little. Although he was grateful that he was not alone, he was sure that night would fall within minutes and the darkness would be absolute.

Finally, the rain had stopped. The air was cool. It was still a bit cloudy, and the night sky was no help for navigation. Tom never questioned Quan's ability to get him home because she had shepherded both he and Grandpa home before. Tom did not recognize the lay of the land before it got too dark to see. Now, he was completely dependent upon Quan. He could not see her properly, but he could make out her shape against the ground clutter. He also discovered that he could hear her quite well.

He was aching all over, but his ankle was of particular distress. He tolerated the pain, but he knew from his brother's sport activities that if he rested, his ankle would stiffen up in no time. As much as he wanted to stop and rest, he slowly pressed onward. The growing rawness of his hands told him that he would not be able to hold on to the stick much longer anyway. As soon as that thought crossed his mind, a small tear in the palm of his left hand ripped open. A blister had rubbed raw and torn open.

Tom stood there and wondered what to do. He had no bandages. Everything he had on was soaked in nonsterile water or flat-out dirty. He stuck the flap of skin back over the wound and put his finger over it. He stood there, holding his hand above his head and counted to one hundred. He figured that would be enough time to stop the bleeding. However, he realized that he could no longer use the walking stick. He also noted that in the time he had stood there, his left ankle had indeed stiffened up on him. Tom tried to hop on just his right leg, but that lasted for only about five hops before he understood the futility of his efforts.

Tom collapsed to the ground and laid on his right side. He was too exhausted to scream, cry, yell, or moan. He just lay on the ground and stared at the horizontal layers of grass in front of him. They reminded him of tiny jail cell bars. Quan came and stood by him for a few minutes. When he didn't move to pet her, she came over and nudged his hand. He gave her three scratches on her ear and then returned his hand to its previous resting spot. Quan turned in a circle twice and then lay down next to him. She let out a sigh, as if to let him know how much she felt sorry for him.

With more than a hint of sarcasm, Tom said aloud, "Every day, and in every way, I am getting better and better." Exhausted, scared, and with a certain degree of surrender, Tom closed his eyes. Within minutes, he was asleep.

Quan lay next to him and listened to him breath. She knew his smell from a quarter mile away. He had a distinctive emerald smell. It was a smell she had never known before and enjoyed being close to it. She saw Tom as the human equivalent of a puppy. He had a great energy and a playfulness that the other did not. She saw William as a mix of the alpha male and a human friend. The love she had for them both was unmistakable, but this one was fun to be around. Now, she was concerned because he was hurt.

Earlier in the day, Quan smelled the storm coming and went looking for the Jeep. When she got there, it had been empty but the emerald smell was definitely there. However, the rain and wind did not help her at all. The deep, dark green scent of Tom was fading fast as the rain washed it away. It was becoming pastel, and, finally, it started to disappear altogether. Quan followed it to the water and to the log. She jumped at the same place Tom jumped, but she made it across. There the trail had grown cold. Just as she decided to go back to the house, she heard Tom yell. When she got to him, she was excited because she thought he was just lost. Now, she knew he was hurt and scared. Those emotions had colors too. Once Tom was asleep, she took off for the house.

Sid was awaiting his dinner. He figured something was up since the Jeep was missing, but he waited on the porch to see what would happen. When Quan called out to him in the distance, he bolted into the woods and quickly found her. She led Sid back to where Tom was. He, too, knew the emerald smell. Although Sid was more aloof, he knew the smell of fear and pain. He took off at a gallop and headed to the closest house. It wasn't home, but it would have to do.

Tom woke up some time later because he thought he heard a motor. He struggled to sit up and then listened. There was a motor off in the distance but it did not sound like the Jeep at all. He also couldn't tell where the sound was coming from.

"Quan," Tom called out weakly.

He called her name a few more times, but she was not within hearing distance. Tom was trying to decide whether it was a good idea to be loud so that someone would find him or to be quiet so that some *thing* would *not* find him. Suddenly, the barking in the distance told Tom exactly what was going on. Quan had found Grandpa and was bringing him there. Tom tried to stand up and immediately regretted it. The various pains in his body all shouted in chorus. He stayed seated and tried to remain patient.

Within a few minutes, Tom was surprised to see both Quan and Sid come through the grass to greet him. A few seconds later, a light could be seen bouncing toward them. Finally, a man on a four-wheeled utility vehicle pulled into the clearing. Once the motor was silenced, the man took off his helmet and shined the headlight in Tom's direction.

"Is that you, William?" asked the voice in the darkness.

"No, I'm Tom ... Tom Miller. I'm his grandson," said Tom.

"I'm Felipe Lopez. I'm your neighbor. What do you say we get you someplace warm and dry?"

"I'm all for it," said Tom.

Felipe walked over to Tom and flashed him a warm smile. He offered Tom a hand getting up and noticed that he was looking for his makeshift cane.

"Hold on a second," said Felipe.

Seeing Tom up close, he saw how he was dressed and the trail of blood that ran down his arm and hand. He scooped up Tom into his strong arms and placed him on the back of the vehicle. A press of the starter button and it roared to life. With a canine escort, they headed toward Felipe's home.

Chapter 14 – Chrysalis

Tom kept his eyes closed for most of the trip. The day had exhausted him, and he just wanted it to be over. As much as he wanted to fall asleep, the rumble of the motor, the bumpy ride, and an occasional jolt of pain were not conducive for rest. Tom hung on and waited for it to be over. Shortly, an A-frame cabin appeared in the darkness. He had seen these before in travel brochures that his parents had lying around the house. It looked like a small ski lodge.

As they came closer to the cabin, Tom could make out two silhouetted figures standing in front. From the looks of it, Felipe had a wife and daughter. As they pulled up to the house, the wife had a look of worry that changed to dismay. The daughter just looked stunned, as if they had just appeared from out of the sky. Once the motor was off, Quan came up to Tom and was wagging her tail as if to say, "See what I did!" and put her paws up on Tom's knee. Tom gave her a scratch behind the ear.

"Good girl, Quan. You are absolutely a lifesaver," said Tom.

Quan gave him a couple of licks on the chin and then sat down a few feet from him.

"What happened?" shouted Felipe's wife.

"He's banged up a bit, dear. Let's get him in and cleaned up. He's William's grandson," said Felipe.

"Hi, there. Tom Miller. I've had a hard day," was all Tom could think to say at that moment.

The daughter turned and opened the door. Felipe put Tom's left arm over his shoulder and helped him to his feet.

"What's wrong with him?" asked Felipe's wife as she moved to the door.

"Well, I'm guessing he has hurt his ankle. The cuts and scrapes on his hands and face are from making his way out of the woods," said Felipe.

Felipe continued to support him as they hobbled to the doorway. His wife had gone inside, and his daughter still stood with the door open. As they lurched through the doorway, Tom muttered a thank you to the girl and then looked inside. Tom thought he must be seeing double as he saw about a dozen computers in the front room. A few of them were working, but most were in various stages of repair.

Out from the hallway to the right, Felipe's wife came out of the bathroom. He could hear water running in the tub as though she was going to take a bath. Tom thought it was an awfully odd time to be taking a bath until he noticed that she was carrying towels for him. Felipe had Tom sit in an old office chair that was in the midst of the computers. Felipe's wife covered him up with a couple of towels.

"I know that you have to be cold. Put these around you, sweetie," said Felipe's wife.

"Thank you," said Tom, as he did what he was instructed.

"OK, pick up your feet," said Felipe.

Not knowing what else to do, Tom picked up his feet. Felipe started to wheel him to the bathroom.

"Oh," said Tom as he saw where this was going.

Felipe rolled Tom into the bathroom and then closed the door. He bent over and checked the water flow to make sure it was still warm. He also checked the water in the tub. It, too, was warm.

"Can you balance on one foot?" asked Felipe.

"Yeah, I think so," answered Tom.

"All right then, get yourself undressed and into the tub. Once you're in the tub, give me a shout so I can get your clothes into the wash."

Tom nodded his head. Felipe stepped out and Tom started wiggling out of his clothes. He could hear both wife and daughter peppering Felipe with questions as they retreated down the hall. Tom had a lopsided grin as he heard the phrase *I don't know* over and over. After getting undressed, he stood up on his right foot, pivoted to the tub and, sat down. He pivoted again and slid down into the warm water. Felipe's wife was kind enough to sit out a set of wash cloths and towels. She even put bath salts in the tub. Tom wasn't sure what bath salts were, but they smelled nice ... exactly the opposite of the way he did. However, any place he had a scratch, he felt a slight burning sensation.

There was a tap on the door.

"Yes?" asked Tom.

A female voice responded, "Can I get your clothes now?"

"Uh ... yeah. I guess," said Tom.

Tom pulled the curtain closed around the tub as the bathroom door opened. He heard the sound of clothes being thrown into a basket.

"Thank you. Again," said Tom.

Without a word, Felipe's daughter gathered up the soggy, torn clothing and closed the door. Tom realized that he had been holding his breath and finally exhaled. Here he had been soaked by rain, pummeled by hail, nearly drowned, and lost in the woods, and a girl on the other side of the tub curtain made him hold his breath. He realized the ludicrous moment for what it was, laughed, and finished washing.

When Tom had finished his bath, he opened the drain to let the dirt, twigs and leaves go down the drain. Once he had the tub filled again, he really got himself cleaned up. He then borrowed one of his mom's tricks and rolled up the washcloth, placed it behind his neck and stretched out. Again, he released a contented sigh as he realized he was out of harm's way. A few minutes later, another tap was heard at the door.

"Yes?" asked Tom.

"Is it alright if I come in?"

"Sure, I guess," answered Tom as he opened the curtain a bit.

Felipe came in and sat down on the chair. He had a kind face that was framed by dark hair, dark eyes, and ivory teeth. Still, his good looks were diminished by his wrinkles of concern.

"Are you feeling better now?"

"Absolutely! Thank you, and thank you for finding me. How did you manage that?" asked Tom.

"Well, it was kind of strange. We see the dogs every once in a while and know that they belong to your grandfather, but they don't ever come up to the house. I was going about my business when I heard a dog bark in the yard. Since that storm had just passed through, I thought that maybe something had happened to William. So, I got a jacket, a cell phone, and a flashlight and headed toward his place," said Felipe.

A small stream of water dribbled out of the tub's faucet, interrupting his story. Tom reached up to tighten the faucet handles and then Felipe continued.

"The dog kept leading me away from his place though. He kept heading for the back of *my* property. This was quite strange, but I figured that it knew more than I did. I followed for about five hundred yards or so until I saw the other dog. This one started running around in circles and bouncing around, you know. I knew then, for sure, that they were leading me to something. I was still thinking that I was going to find William," said Felipe.

"So I guess you were just as surprised to find me as I was seeing you," said Tom.

"Definitely. I didn't know William had company, so seeing anyone other than William was a surprise. Do you know where he is?" asked Felipe.

"He went into town to meet with some investors or something like that. I know he was going to the shop, giving a tour, and then going out to dinner. I thought about staying with the Jeep, thinking that he'd find me later. But, with the Jeep dead, a storm coming, and dogs needing to be fed, I knew that I needed to head back to the house. Later, I realized that the storm would slow Grandpa down since he was on his motorcycle," said Tom.

"A motorcycle? I didn't know he rode," said Felipe with a look of surprise.

"Neither did I until today. I'm learning a lot about my grandpa since being up here … especially today."

"Well, while you were in the tub, I called over there to see if he was home. I got an answering machine, so at least the power is working again. I left him a message to let him know you're here. I told him, that given the hour and the fact he wasn't home, that you'd be staying here for the evening and that we'd bring you back tomorrow," said Felipe.

"Thank you," said Tom.

"Also, while I thought of it, I gave the dogs some hamburgers we had left over from a couple of nights ago."

"Thank you, again. That is very nice of you. I probably should be polite and say I should be getting home, but I am really feeling beaten up," said Tom honestly.

"Don't worry about it. We were going to drop by today, but the weather report kept us here. Dropping you off tomorrow will be no problem," said Felipe.

141

Felipe stood up and moved toward the door.

"When you're done there, my wife has made something for you to eat. I'm sure you've not had much today. I'll leave the chair so you can roll back out."

"Thanks again," said Tom, "I'll be out in a second."

A few minutes later, Tom slowly got out of the tub and tested his ankle. It was still pretty sore, but he could limp where he needed to go. He found a red flannel robe draped across the chair, so he put it on, toweled off his hair, and moved to turn off the light and leave the room.

He had to stare at the mirror for a second to see who was looking back at him. It was and wasn't his face looking back at him. He had a nasty scratch under his left eye and a few more scattered across his face. But the thing he stared at the most was his eyes. The eyes that stared back at him were different; they were darker somehow. He stared for a few seconds and tried to fathom the newfound depths. Eventually, he shrugged and thought that he was just tired. He turned off the light and went to meet the neighbors wearing nothing more than a robe and a tired smile.

Tom used the chair for support and slowly walked out of the bathroom. He rounded the corner of the hall and entered into the great room. Again, he was amazed to see so many computers in one location. He looked the opposite direction and saw a kitchen. Everyone was sitting around the table but there was only one place setting. He moved the rolling chair over and sat down. His eyes darted back and forth at the three sets of curious brown eyes looking back at him and the food in front of him.

"We want to ask you a bunch of questions, but we know you're probably famished. Are burritos OK with you? If not, I can make you a grilled cheese sandwich or something else," said Felipe's wife.

"No, burritos are great with me. I really do appreciate all the kindness you have shown me. You have all been really cool," said Tom.

Tom looked at his plate and thought everything appeared delicious—especially the black beans and rice. Food, warmth, and companionship were all Tom needed.

"If you don't mind me talking with my mouth full, I don't mind talking while I eat," said Tom.

"Well, get started then," said Felipe, as he pushed a jar of salsa toward Tom.

Tom was a little bashful, at first, with everyone looking at him. His stomach urged him onward, and soon he was eating burritos, tortilla chips with guacamole dip, and anything else that was in arm's reach.

Soon, the questions started coming, and Tom did his best to answer them and eat at the same time. How long have you been at your grandfather's house? Where are you from? Do you have any brothers or sisters? What were you doing in the woods? Why are you digging up trees?

"Is William teaching you memory pegs too?" asked Felipe's daughter as she tucked her long black hair behind her ear.

"Memory pegs? What's that?" asked Tom.

"It's a game that William taught me where you can learn things and keep them in your mind by connecting them to things you already have memorized," answered Felipe's daughter.

"For example, for the letter T, my peg is a tomato. Your name is Tom and I imagine

you eating a tomato. Now I have both a word and a picture to remember your name."

"Don't suppose you eat hummus?" asked Tom wryly.

"Huh?" replied the girl.

"Never mind ... I never heard of memory pegs. I think Grandpa has been teaching me to question the answers. For example, I thought that Columbus discovered North America. Actually, he discovered the East Coast of some South American countries. The Vikings were the first to discover North America," said Tom.

"Interesting. What else is he teaching you?" asked Felipe.

"He is teaching me a bunch of things. I guess the best way to sum it up is that he is teaching me to pay more attention to the world around me. Instead of just letting things happen to me, I should look forward and be positive in what I do and say," said Tom.

"Those are very good things to know. As soon as you learn that you are the master of your own fate, the sooner you can chart a course for yourself," said Felipe.

They continued talking for a while longer. Felipe was a computer repair technician who worked for a couple of different companies. He would repair the computers sent to him and send them back to the company. The company would then send them back to the employees. Felipe's wife was Elena. She was a housewife, a business partner, and a teacher. Their daughter was Serafina—Sera for short. She was a year younger than Tom but stood about three inches taller than he was. They had moved up from Mexico City almost ten years earlier. In spite of being here that long, though, Sera had never been to school. Her mother had taught her at home. As such, Sera spoke both English and Spanish and knew a lot about computers.

Soon Tom's stomach was full and his tongue was tired. Everyone's curiosity was temporarily satisfied, and the evening's activities left everyone feeling sleepy. No sooner did Tom lay on the couch with a blanket and pillow then he fell asleep. He was snoring lightly when his grandpa called five minutes later.

Chapter 15 – Partnerships

William had a full day that day. He had arrived fifteen minutes before the meeting was supposed to happen so that he could chat with the shop foreman and refamiliarize himself with the client's wants and needs. However, as he pulled up, on his 1950 Indian Chief motorcycle, a man jumped out of his car and waved him over. The man was absolutely amazed to see such an icon of U.S. history still on the road and looking so good. After a few minutes of chatting with this stranger, William realized that this was the client that he was supposed to be meeting. The discussion about the restoration of the Chief was carried from the parking lot to the meeting room.

Finally, they got down to business. The builder had two different kitchen designs that his company used on a regular basis. However, the occasional homeowner had special requests with regards to the cabinetry. Sometimes, the special requests would increase as the homeowner wanted additional custom cabinetry in other rooms. William and his team convinced the builder to consider variations of what his company already produced, including using reclaimed lumber and bamboo. Eventually, they came to an agreement to provide seven stock sets to complement the different kitchen designs. William also provided the builder with a specialized catalog of built-in bookcases, armoires, and entertainment centers that his company had previously designed for other clients.

After the meeting, William wanted to take everyone to dinner. Because he did not come in to work very often, he liked to take the employees out to dinner when he had the chance. He liked to get to know them and to make sure they knew that he appreciated them. Much of the dinner conversation again returned to the motorcycle, but once the builder left, William did get to spend some time with his employees. By the time everyone had eaten, visited, and headed for home, it was both late and raining. A couple of his employees offered to take him home but William declined, knowing it was out of the way for them.

Anyone who has ridden a motorcycle knows that if it rains, the roads will be slick ... not just from water, but from all the fluids that accumulate on the roadway during ordinary use. What develops is a thin film of a slick mixture known as black ice. Another concern is cars. Cars have more than twice the surface area for traction and have a lot more weight than motorcycles have. It never ceases to amaze most motorcycle riders that when the roads become more hazardous, people who drive the "safer" cars become more reckless. It's not a good combination for those who have to ride motorcycles in the rain.

One thing that made matters worse for William was that the Chief did not have the customary shifter that many motorcycle riders are accustomed to using. Instead of using your left foot to shift, you used a large lever located on the left hand side of the gas tank. This lever, which looks like the gear shifter from a tractor trailer, is affectionately known as a suicide clutch. In weather like this, it was best not to steer with one hand.

William decided to wait out the storm and ride home in about an hour. However, while he waited in the restaurant, he overheard some others talking about the tornado that had been spotted close to where he lived. William immediately called home to see if Tom was safe. Tom did not answer. William became increasingly worried but made himself wait a bit longer to see if the rain would subside. Finally, William decided to ride back to the office, leave the Chief in the warehouse, and use one of the company trucks to get home. Once at the shop, William called home again only to discover the power was off since the answering machine did not pick up, and, still, no one was home.

It took more time than he thought to find the keys, but, eventually, William was on the road and heading for home. He tried to call from his cell phone, but he had forgotten to charge the phone in a while and now it was useless. William tossed the phone onto the passenger seat in disgust and drove a little faster. It was close to 10:00 p.m. when he finally pulled up to his house. He knew there was trouble when he drove up: No lights were on in the house, no Jeep was in the drive, and the dogs were nowhere to be seen.

William hurried into the house, turned on the light in the kitchen, and saw that nothing had changed since breakfast. He was becoming more scared. He knew that he needed to give Tom the opportunity to discover his mettle by learning self-reliance, but had he pushed him too hard too soon? William sat down at the kitchen table and calmed his mind. Soon, the fear and worry faded from his mind. An image of a room full of computers popped into his head. He had seen that room before. He picked up the phone and called his neighbor. When he heard from Felipe, he cried, as both relief and empathy washed over him.

Later that night, William was dreaming of being in a forest and having a conversation with his elderly Indian guide. Of course, the discussion was about Tom.

"I'm not pushing him too fast, am I?" asked a worried William.

"No. He is ready for this, and there are those who guide him from this place too", answered William's spirit guide. As he sat on a large rock, a sunbeam appeared in his lap where his folded hands rested.

"Thank you, Grandfather ... thank you, Little Eagle," said William as he drifted deeper into sleep.

Little Eagle smiled the smile of someone who already knows the answer to a question.

He deliberately turned his wrinkled but strong hands over catch the sunlight as though it was water.

The early morning sun was persistent in its attempt to wake Tom up. Tom tried to turn over and face away from the window, but his body instantly began berating him for his mistreatment. He lay on the couch and mentally worked his way from his toes to his scalp. He discovered that his toes, his right earlobe, and his hair were the only things on his body that didn't hurt. He needed some of his grandpa's mojo if he was going to get up off the couch. He tried to reposition himself several times before he finally decided just to get up.

He flipped back the covers and slowly slid his legs over the side of the couch and onto the floor. He was still quite tired but figured that he should get up and call his grandpa to make sure that he was not freaking out. He glanced into the kitchen and saw Elena and Sera moving around. He smiled when he noticed that they both had on pink fuzzy slippers. He had started to stand up when he realized that he was wearing the same robe from last night. The only difference from last night was that the robe had come open. With a rush of adrenaline and embarrassment, Tom whipped the robe around him and tied it closed. As he looked up, he noticed that the ladies were both looking at him inquisitively.

"Uh ... good morning," said Tom.

"Good morning!" they said in cheerful unison.

"How did you sleep?" asked Sera.

"I don't feel like I slept at all. I feel as though I just closed my eyes and then it was morning," said Tom.

"Well, you really needed to sleep more than six or seven hours," said Elena.

"You need to tell that to my dad. He is always telling me that I sleep too much," said Tom.

"Teenagers need to sleep to help them adjust to all the growing that they do. But you shouldn't sleep the day away either," said Elena.

Standing behind her mother, Sera rolled her eyes and shook her head as though she couldn't believe these words were coming out of her mother's mouth. Tom saw this and couldn't help but smile. Looking back at Tom, Sera smiled too.

"Oh, your grandpa called a few minutes after you laid down on the couch last night. He was very relieved to hear that you were here and resting well. We told him that we were going to be coming over this morning, so he invited us to have breakfast with him," said Elena.

"That sounds fine to me. I have to ask though, why did Felipe say that you had planned on coming over yesterday?" inquired Tom.

"Well, we made a batch of muffins yesterday, and I wanted to take them over while they were still fresh," answered Sera.

"Oh, man, are you the ones who Grandpa gets the wild berry muffins from? Those things are fantastic!" said Tom enthusiastically.

Both of them smiled back at Tom with appreciation.

"Yes, I pick the berries, and then Mom and I make them for us and for William," said Sera.

"You guys need to bag them up and sell them to a grocery store. I know they would fly right off the shelves," said Tom.

"It's always nice to hear a compliment," said Elena, "However, I do need to get moving. I need to get to the store and get some supplies for Felipe."

Elena emerged from the kitchen with a small box of muffins and an ice pack for Tom's ankle. She sat the box next to him and handed him the ice pack. Sera came out with a tall glass of milk and a couple of aspirin.

Tom looked up at Elena first and then at Sera and said, "Did I mention how much I appreciate how wonderful you guys are?"

Tom gratefully took the ice pack and put it on his ankle. The aspirin and milk found their way to his stomach. Elena went back down the hall and finished getting ready to run errands. Sera went back to the kitchen and returned with two muffins and another glass of milk. She handed Tom a muffin and then sat down adjacent to him.

"So, how soon do you want to leave?" asked Sera.

"Um, I guess when I have some clothes," said Tom honestly.

Sera giggled, "Oh, man, I forgot to bring them out here."

Sera bounded down the hall—a flash of ebony hair and pink slippers. It made Tom smile. He noticed the blue pajamas with teddy bears in sleeping caps as she brought back Tom's clothes.

"There are a couple of tears in your T-shirt. My mom wanted to fix them but Dad thought you would want to keep them as a souvenir," said Sera.

"Yeah, I guess there's a good story in there. Right now, it's a little too close to see it that way," said Tom.

"Well, Dad's in the shower and Mom is fussing with her make-up. I am going to go get dressed and then we can head out of here," said Sera, who got up and was down the hall before he could say another word.

He felt a bit self-conscious about getting dressed in the main room of a house of people he had just met. Not wanting to burden his ankle more than necessary, he went through a series of contortions to get dressed without surprising anyone and without hurting himself too much. As he was putting on his shoes, Felipe came out of the back wearing a robe and three small pieces of tissue on his chin and face.

"I'm telling you, Tom, enjoy not having to shave while you can. Once you start you can never go back. Oh, by the way, good morning," said Felipe.

"Good morning," said Tom with a grin.

"Sorry I can't chat, but I am late for a meeting," said Felipe.

Tom watched Felipe sit down at a computer, type in a few letters and then walk into the kitchen and pour a cup of coffee. He then went back to the computer and typed in a few more letters. Then, to Tom's surprise, he stood up, untied his robe and let it slide to the floor. Thankfully, he was wearing jogging shorts. He pulled a dress shirt from the back of the chair and put it on. As he finished putting on his shirt, the computer spoke.

"Password?" asked a female voice from the computer.

"Progress," answered Felipe.

"Your name please?" asked the computer.

"Felipe Lopez," answered Felipe.

Felipe reached on top of his computer monitor and grabbed a fake tie—one that gets clipped on instead of tied into a knot. He clipped on his tie, folded his collar, and smoothed back his hair as the light on his webcam turned on.

"Ah, Philip, glad you could join us. What time is it there?"

This was a staff meeting for the company Felipe contracted with for employment. He knew that Rob, the moron manager, on the other end, knew perfectly well that it was about 7:30 a.m. where he was and that his name was not Philip. He also insisted Felipe take part in video conferencing even though he would have nothing to say for fifty minutes. Felipe would speak for only about five minutes, at the very end, to report his progress. It was something he could do easily via e-mail, but Felipe was sure that Rob wanted to justify having his own webcam and any other toys the company would let him get away with keeping.

Pretending to take notes, Felipe wrote a note to Tom, telling him to take care and to come back and visit anytime he wanted. He also asked that William give him a call later. Tom gingerly got up and slowly made his way to the desk. Off camera, Tom read the note and gave Felipe the OK sign. Tom heard the front door open and saw Sera, with the box of muffins, waving him out the door. Tom waved goodbye to Felipe and quietly made his way out the door.

Outside the air was cool, and the dew still glistened on the grass and trees. The sun was already even with the treetops and gave the hillside a golden glow. Sera strapped the box and the tarp to the front of the ATV and handed Tom a helmet.

"Not that I am a bad driver, but Dad says we always need to wear one of these," said Sera.

"After yesterday, I am through risk-taking for a little while," said Tom.

Sera looked at him for a second, as if she wanted to say something. She thought better of it, put her own helmet on, and started the vehicle. It rumbled to life immediately and then they were off.

William heard them before he saw them. He had not slept well that night. It was a dreamless sleep where he kept waking up every hour or so. Finally, a little before sunrise, he decided he wasn't getting sleep today. He did a few minutes of tai chi to stretch and focus. He then meditated for about twenty minutes to feel more energetic. After that, he was out to the kitchen yo begin his coffee ritual. As he was having his first cup of coffee and staring out at the sunrise, he heard Quan and Sid barking and then taking off across the property. Company would soon arrive.

William saw the ATV pull up and went out to greet them. He smiled to see Sera. His smile was somewhat artificial as Tom took off his helmet. Tom had scratches all over his face, but the one under his eye looked particularly painful.

"Hola, William," said Sera.

"Buenos días, Señorita Lopez. ¿Cómo está usted?" asked William.

"Muy bien, gracias. I have brought you a gift."

"Yes, indeed you have. Hello, Thomas, what's new with you?" asked William with a bona fide grin.

"Oh, not much, I got rained upon, hailed upon, nearly drowned, twisted my ankle, scratched up my hands, and had the river treat my head as if it were a piñata," said Tom.

"Hmm, other than that?" asked William.

"Oh, I met some really nice people," said Tom and looked at Sera.

"Well, let's go in and have something to eat, and each of us can tell our tales," said William.

Chapter 16 – Dreams

William led them into the kitchen, where they munched on muffins and shared their tales of the day before. The weather had interrupted the day for both of them yesterday, but today was bright, sunny, and welcoming—a new beginning. Sera sat, rapt with attention, as Tom went into more detail about his troubles with his grandpa than he had with the Lopez family. William listened with more than a bit of awe and respect for his grandson's resilience. At the same time, he felt a pang of guilt. He was sure Tom wouldn't have had to endure so much pain if he had told him to stay home. But he knew that he needed to give Tom the opportunity to discover his own dormant strengths. This was the delicate balance every parent knew.

William summed up Tom's story with the comment, "Tom, that was the best story of intestinal fortitude I have heard in a long time."

"Intestinal fortitude?" asked Tom, "It sounds like you're describing someone who can eat anything."

Sera and Tom laughed in unison.

"OK, you sure do have some guts ... how about that?" asked William with his trademark grin.

"Thanks, Grandpa," said Tom with visible pride.

"Well, Sera, since you have brought the ATV, would you mind taking Tom back to the Jeep so he can bring it back to the house?" asked William.

"Sure, no problem. How are we going to start it if it has a dead battery?" asked Sera.

"Oh, I have a little toy in the garage that will allow you to jump-start it," said William.

William explained how to use the portable battery charger, and Sera and Tom were off again on the ATV. William's battery charger looked something like a small yellow suitcase. Inside was a battery and cables to attach to the Jeep's battery to get it running again. Tom was surprised that Grandpa was willing to go let him go out into the woods again to get the Jeep. He was sure that if William had been his dad, he would have made Tom stay home while he went and took care of it. The fact that his grandpa trusted him to do this made him feel much more mature.

When they crossed the creek bed, it was fairly muddy but passable. The gentle stream of water that ran there now was but a shadow of its former self. Sera had fun going through it. She hit the throttle as they crossed it and sent mud flying. They both yelled with delight as they continued to the Jeep. Once there, getting the vehicle started was just as simple as William had described. Within the hour, they were pulling up to the house again. They parked their respective vehicles and entered the house through the garage. They met William in the library.

"Good, you guys are back. Any problems?" asked William.

"Nope, everything went just as you described, Grandpa," said Tom.

"Sera, might I ask a favor of you?" inquired William.

"Sure. What's up?" asked Sera.

"Tom has some lessons and some reading to do. Would you be willing to hang out here and give him a hand where he needs it? I have to spend a few hours in my office today and can't hover over him as much as I would like," said William.

"I don't see any reason why not. I should check with my parents first to make sure it's OK," said Sera.

"Excellent. Felipe called to see if you both were safe and sound. I asked him if you could stay and he said yes, for as long as you want," said William.

"Cool," said Tom and Sera at the same time.

"All right then, before I go to work I have a small lesson for you both," said William as he gestured them into the classroom. There were two chairs, two desks, and two bottles of water. One desk, however, had a small cup with capsules in it. To Tom, it looked like crushed oregano.

"That happens to be an herbal concoction I put together from some of my plants growing upstairs. They will address any aches and pains you have going on," said William, answering Tom's unspoken question.

Once everyone was comfortable, William walked over to the dry erase board. He wrote the following:

"Chances are that both of you, at one time or another, have dreamt that you were flying or falling. Chances are that you have dreamt that you were driving or riding in a vehicle from one place to another. Does any of this sound familiar to you?"

Tom and Sera nodded their heads in unison, and William continued.

"Also, you may have been to a place, or in a situation, that you have not previously experienced. Suddenly, while you are in the situation, a sense of familiarity washes over you," said William.

Again, they nodded their heads in unison, but Sera's eyes grew large.

"Then there is a good chance that you have experienced something called precognition. It is when you are going about your day and then you suddenly feel like you have been there before but in reality you have not. Sound familiar?"

"Oh, my gosh, I can't believe that you said that!" exclaimed Sera.

"Why do you say that?" asked William.

"I had a dream the night before last that some kid was sitting outside in my yard. I did not recognize him but I was not scared of him either. It seemed weird because we live pretty far out from town. Strangers don't show up at our place, you know?" said Sera.

"Yes," answered William, "Go on."

"Anyway, it was even weirder because I thought the kid in my dream was wearing what one of those things Roman guys would wear," said Sera.

"You mean a toga?" asked William.

"Yeah, one of those," said Sera.

"Interesting that you would have had a dream about Tom before you met him," said William.

"What does that mean?" asked Tom.

"The person who is probably most qualified to answer that question is Sera," answered William.

"I don't know what it means," said Sera.

"Well, maybe it will come to you later, but you dream about things for a reason. So let me tell you a bit about dreams."

"Grandpa, I have a quick question. Why did Sera dream about me in a toga? I was wearing a tarp," said Tom.

"Well, I would have to speculate that Sera is familiar with the concept of a toga. When she dreamt the image of you wearing a tarp, her brain associated the image with the concept of toga. Remember your associations with hummus?" asked William.

"Oh, right," said Tom.

"I can tell you that if I would have dreamt about a stranger in my yard wearing a tarp, I would have freaked out. It reminds me of a scary Halloween movie I saw a while back," said Sera.

"Given the association she has with the tarp imagery, can you see why she thought of a toga instead?" asked William.

"Yeah, I guess she would have been really scared, otherwise, when I showed up," said Tom.

"Indeed," said William, "Now let's move on with dream control."

Tom and Sera shared an excited glance at each other and then looked back to William.

"Dreams are very important to your development as a person. Studies have been done to confirm that people who are prevented from dreaming for prolonged periods end up becoming physically and/or mentally ill. Luckily, these effects are temporary and go away once the person is allowed to dream again."

"One of the most prevalent beliefs about dreaming is that it allows the conscious and the subconscious to process the day's events. Although your focus may be on a particular event or subject, your subconscious is picking up data from all of your senses. When the conscious mind can rest from the day of acquiring information, it can work with the subconscious to store or delete information."

"Sometimes, you may have a problem with a school project or a relationship where you have really worked hard at finding a solution, but there was no immediate answer. If you allow your conscious and your subconscious mind to work on it together, a solution usually presents itself," said William.

"Is that why you hear people say that they're going to 'sleep on it'?" asked Tom.

"It's as good as any other reason I've heard," said William.

"My dad does that sometimes. He will be working on a problem on someone's computer, and when he can't think of an answer, he gets frustrated. He will tell everyone he is going to take a nap. When he gets up from his nap, he almost always has an answer," volunteered Sera.

"People have been using their minds like this for centuries, but I have never heard it taught in a school yet. Then again, there is a lot that should be in school that isn't," said William.

"Right now, I want to consider this metaphor. You can move from house to house throughout your life but will probably never build a house of your own—one specific to your needs, wishes, and dreams. However, a smaller number of people have done exactly that. Right now, you have become aware that you can move ideas around in your mind just like moving boxes from one house to another. Remember that you have the capacity to be an active participant where your mind is concerned. You need not be passive observers in your dreams. You can build and manipulate variables in your mind just as another may build their house from the ground up. The best part is that not only is there zero impact to the environment, it costs nothing to do and you can do it every day of your life."

"My mom says that when she was a little girl, she used to travel places while she was asleep. Have you heard anything about that?" asked Sera.

"Well, assuming that she was not referring to the fact that she was asleep in a car while someone was driving, I would guess that she was talking about astral projection," said William.

"What's that?" asked Tom.

"I have not read too much about it, but as I understand it, astral projection is when you pick out a place that you wish to travel to before you go to sleep. Once you go to sleep, a part of your consciousness is able to leave your body and travel to wherever ... or maybe whenever you so desire," said William.

"How many parts does your consciousness have, Grandpa?" asked Tom.

"Tom, if you could definitively answer that question, you could be a millionaire. I read somewhere that there is a subconscious, a conscious, and a superconscious. When you have a free moment, have a look at any of the books I have from Edgar Cayce," said William.

"Casey who?" asked Tom.

"Edgar Cayce ... C-A-Y-C-E. As far as who he was, he was a psychic. As far as what that really means, I will leave that for you to discover. I will tell you that he was an amazing individual who received information in an unusual way. People thought he was crazy until science finally caught up with him," said William.

William thought for a second. Cayce would make a good transition point.

"Of course, Cayce obtained information while he was in a light trance state. One of the nicknames he had was the Sleeping Prophet. Now, let's talk about what I want you to do while you are asleep this evening," said William.

"What kind of information did he get?" asked Tom.

William allowed the digression and answered, "He received different kinds of information. Sometimes it was for a specific person; sometimes it was for people in general. Come to think of it, there are thousands of pages of information that he communicated. However, we are drifting from the lesson I have planned for you."

"OK, what's the lesson?" asked Sera enthusiastically.

"The lesson is this. Tomorrow I am going to do an experiment in the barn. I want you to dream about the experiment tonight. See yourself standing in front of the barn with the doors open and look inside. Then I want you to write down what you see on a piece of paper when you wake up. Fold the paper up and then tape it closed. Tomorrow we will see who was able to see into the future," said William.

"That sounds cool," said Sera.

"That sounds cool if it works," said Tom.

"There is another thing I want you to do. I want you to pick a time to wake up tomorrow morning. Pick a specific time and tell yourself that you are going to wake up at that time as you are going to sleep," said William.

"You can do that?" asked Tom.

"Of course you can," said William.

"I would never get up if I didn't set my alarm," said Tom.

"Have you ever told yourself to be up at a specific time while going to sleep?" asked Sera.

"No," said Tom.

"Well then ...," said Sera in a smug tone. William chuckled.

"On that note, I think we will call it quits for the classroom," said William.

With that being said, William escorted them to the library. He gestured for them to sit down and then walked over to the shelf closest to the window and pulled two books from it. Returning to Tom, he handed him the books.

"I have taken the liberty of getting a couple of books for you so that you can rest your ankle. I still want you to tell me who invented the radio. I have a book here on inventors, and I have another that is about a man named Nicola Tesla. From these two books, you can come up with a report that we can discuss over dinner," said William.

Tom nodded absently, as he was already engrossed in the book about Tesla. He knew it was one of Grandpa's heroes and it was the same one he had seen earlier. He saw the same huge pillar with a silver bowl of lightning. Flipping through it, he discovered a picture of Tesla. Tom was struck by how regal he looked in the picture.

William then turned his attention to Sera and handed her a slip of paper.

"Sera, here's the number to the phone in the barn. There is a phone in the classroom over on the desk. If you should need anything, give me a ring. I shouldn't be more than four hours. Also, I made a platter of snacks last night and put it in the refrigerator. OK?" asked William.

"Sounds fine to me. Is there anything around here I can do for you since you'll be busy with work stuff?" asked Sera.

"Nope, just look after my apprentice here and make sure he does not tax his ankle anymore," said William as he gently mussed with Tom's hair.

Chapter 17 – Realities

William headed to his office in the barn so that he could do some work and prepare for tomorrow's experiment. Sera watched him leave and then looked at Tom, who was still flipping through the book. She had never spent time in the library before, so she wandered around and took in the sights. She, like Tom, was surprised at the number of books that William had. Since her dad was involved with computers, she looked to see if William had some of the same books that her dad had. He didn't.

She continued to look through the books while occasionally looking over to Tom. Tom was completely absorbed in the book. On one hand, she thought that it was rude of him to ignore her. On the other hand, she was supposed to be looking out for him and not chatting with him. Finally, she decided to find a book on astral projection. She not only found a couple of books about that, but next to them she found books on remote viewing. *This library is like a magic shop*, she thought. Around every corner was something she had never considered before now. It was quite exciting. She finally decided to read a book about people who travel by leaving their bodies. She came back to where Tom was sitting by way of normal ambulation.

Tom had started taking notes on things he read that he felt belonged in a book report. He also wrote down things that he thought were fascinating. As he sat scribbling away, Sera plopped down in the chair adjacent to him. Finishing his thought, Tom looked up.

"Find anything interesting?" asked Tom.

"Everywhere," responded Sera, "Where do you think he got all of these books?"

"Bookstores, I'd imagine," answered Tom.

Sera looked at him as though he were a moron.

"No, no, no ... I mean I guess he got them in stores. I mean, I don't really know where he got them," stammered Tom.

"Apparently, there's quite a bit that you don't know," said Sera a bit aggressively.

Several smart responses quickly came to mind but he took a moment to think before speaking. Realizing that it was all a misunderstanding and remembering what he knew of neurolinguistic programming, Tom came up with a new response.

"That's the absolute truth you got there," replied Tom with a bit of a grin.

Sera blinked and then laughed, which was the exact response Tom was hoping to get. Taking a deep breath of relief, he continued.

"I know that he's my grandfather and all, but he is nothing like I imagined. I mean, he was just Grandpa, the guy who comes to family functions and brings you a neat gift on your birthday. I know it sounds kind of dumb, but I never thought of him as a person," said Tom.

"That sounds weird. Do you think he just sat on a shelf somewhere and jumped up only on specific days?" asked Sera.

"I guess so. I knew facts about him ... he lived alone, he owned a carpentry company, and he liked to tinker and experiment. But the facts sure didn't make up the whole picture. I see how he feels about Sid and Quan, I see how much he enjoys teaching, I see that he is interested in me …," said Tom, his voice trailing off into thought.

"Well, I never knew your grandpa as you describe him. I knew him as this older guy who lived next to us. We met one day while my mother and I were out roaming the edge of our property. He saw that we were collecting raspberries and invited us to come over and do the same on his property. He said that he didn't cook so much so we agreed to bring him something every once in a while. I really liked his smile and his eyes because they were both happy and mischievous. Don't tell him, but my mom and I call him 'El Leprechaun.'"

"Oh man, that's so hilarious and yet so true," said Tom.

"One day when my mom and I came over to drop off some bread and jelly, he and my mom got into a discussion about the U.S. school system, my home schooling, and then about my grades. To make a long story short, William agreed to help me with my English and social studies. Not only did he make it interesting, but he taught me how to make my brain work smarter. He taught me something called memory pegs. With his help, I am almost a year ahead of other kids my age now," said Sera.

"Yeah, he isn't real happy with how schools are run. He is teaching me stuff now that I would never learn in school," said Tom.

"Could you imagine a class on astral projection?" laughed Sera.

"How about a class in mind reading?" joked Tom.

"I wonder how would you cheat on a mind reading exam," giggled Sera.

"When I first got here, Grandpa asked me to think of a word. It was a word that you would not use a whole lot but he picked it right out of the air," said Tom.

"That's cool. Did he teach you?" asked Sera excitedly.

"No, but I know he's teaching me something because I like to eat hummus now and I don't think my brother is as much of a jerk as I used to," said Tom sincerely.

"Do you have any sisters," asked Sera.

"No, just Mom, Dad, and Mark. He just graduated from high school so he thinks he's the king of the world," said Tom.

"That's too bad. When you are on top of the world, the only place to go is down," said Sera.

Tom didn't say anything, but he thought a few seconds about that concept before Sera spoke again.

"Well, I guess that I should let you get back to reading. You need to have something to say to William when he gets back, right?" asked Sera.

"Yeah, I don't want to let him down," said Tom.

They both returned to reading their books. Soon, they were both so engrossed in what they were reading that the hours snuck by, and it was the sound of William upstairs that interrupted them. He shouted from the kitchen to keep reading and he would call them to dinner once it was ready. On they read.

A bit more than an hour later, William announced that dinner was ready. It was one of the more remarkable dinners that either Tom or Sera had ever had. Not because the food was extraordinary, but because the discussion during dinner was.

Astral projection was the first topic of discussion. Sera had read about how different famous Americans had reported out of body experiences. The first person who caught her attention was the author Ernest Hemingway. He was one of the authors who William had introduced to her during their English sessions. Sera was interested to read that while Hemingway was an ambulance driver in World War I, he reported that after a bomb had exploded near him, he felt as if he were floating from his body. He could see himself lying on the ground. He then reported that he could float up and see the battlefield. Just as suddenly, he felt himself pulled back into his own body. He used this incident in his novel *A Farewell To Arms*. One thing that Sera noted in her reading was that, sometimes, people could see an astral traveler.

William added a story about St. Anthony of Padua. St. Anthony was reported to have been in the middle of a sermon when he remembered that he was supposed to be preaching somewhere else. He stopped his sermon and kneeled with his head bowed. St. Anthony then projected himself to the other town. He prayed with the people in the other town for a little while and then disappeared. His astral body returned to his physical body so that he could finish the sermon he had started.

"I can't imagine Christians doing that," said Tom. "Wouldn't they have been fed to the lions or burned at the stake?"

"To the best of my knowledge, the concept of astral projection is all throughout the Old Testament. For example, Elijah used his ability to astral project to travel to the bedroom of a Syrian king and eavesdrop on the king's military plans. Elijah returned with this information and the Israelites survived the Syrian attack."

"Why didn't Elijah teach all of his friends how to do this?" asked Sera.

"That is a good question. If you were afraid of heights, would you like to learn how to skydive? Probably not, because you would be afraid. However, if you were eager to learn and you were willing to challenge your fears, then you might want to give it a try," said William.

"Who else in the bible practiced astral projection?" asked Tom.

"Well, Tom, you have me in an area that I don't know too much about. I can tell you that aside from St. Anthony of Padua, a number of Christians have done it, including St. Ambrose and St. Clement," said William.

"Tell us about what you do know about it," requested Sera.

"Well, I know that it does not belong to any one race, religion, or nationality. I believe the concept in German is referred to as doppelganger. The Scottish refer to it as taslasch, I believe. Astral projection has even been depicted in ancient cave drawings of the Navajo," said William.

Seeing that both Sera and Tom were eager for more information, he took a sip of apple juice and continued.

"I know that in the eighteen hundreds, the American culture lumped it into the concept of Spiritualism. Spiritualists believed that not only could the spirit leave the body on occasion, but that when someone died, the spirit remained intact and was a part of both our plane of existence as well as their own. They were so popular that, by the eighteen fifties, over forty thousand acknowledged Spiritualists lived in New York City alone. Today, Spiritualist camps can still be found—Lily Dale in upstate New York, Cassadaga in Florida, Camp Chesterfield in Indiana," said William.

"Have you ever been to any of these places?" asked Sera.

"I have been to Cassadaga, Camp Chesterfield, and a lovely little church in Sarasota, Florida," said William.

"Did you see any ghosts?" asked Tom excitedly.

"No, no ghosts, no spirits. But I did hear from my grandfather through one of the mediums in Cassadaga. Her name was Lillian, and she was able to confirm my grandfather's name, his physical appearance as I remember it, and his nickname. She told me that I should continue working with my carpentry and I should work just as hard at developing my soul as I did developing my business. She told me that I was the CEO of my soul and that I had to work on my ROI," said William.

Looking at the puzzled faces before him, William added, "ROI is an abbreviation for Return on Investment. Essentially, it means making the most out of what you have been given."

"What about Camp Chesterfield? What was that like?" asked Sera.

"It was like a very small town and college wrapped up into one. The first thing you see is the bookstore, to the right, and the dormitories, to the left. However, there are some very nice homes on the horseshoe-shaped roadway in the camp. I didn't see any spirits there either, but I did go to church," said William.

"Church?" asked Tom.

"Church was pretty interesting. Of course, it had traditional music, readings from the bible and announcements. What was unusual was that there were three different reverends there. They each gave spiritual readings for those in the congregation except in different ways. I found it particularly fascinating that someone I had never met called me by name and then accurately described the emotional and financial state I was in at the time," said William.

Who are some famous spiritualists, Grandpa?" asked Tom.

"Well, I only know of a few ... Charles Lindbergh, of course, Aldous Huxley, and D. H. Lawrence come to mind. Do either of you know who Shirley MacLaine is?"

Tom and Sera shook their heads indicating they did not. Moving along to the next example, William continued.

"The most famous person I know who practiced astral projection," said William returning to the original topic, "was a man named Robert Monroe. He was an ordinary guy who developed his ability of astral travel and then went to extraordinary lengths to quantify his experience. He even recorded what the temperature and humidity was when these events occurred.

"He was both celebrated and demonized for his efforts, as are most who challenge the status quo, but he forged on anyway. He would eventually quit his day job and form the Monroe Institute. Many people today say that his work is the most authoritative to date. Somewhere in my library, I have a copy of his book, *Far Journeys*, if you want to know more about him and his experiences," said William.

Dinner and conversation continued. In between the spaghetti and the meatballs, stories were traded about different movies and stories each knew about people who used astral projection. They talked about the difference between dreams of flying and astral projection and what the difference was between astral projection and remote viewing. Once dinner was concluded, they moved to the front room. William lit a small fire in the fireplace and, once everyone had a seat, William asked Tom what he had learned this afternoon.

"Grandpa, I think Tesla was the best wizard in the world," said Tom.

"Really? I think that you will need to defend a comment that bold," said William as he cleaned his glasses.

"OK, I am only halfway through the first book, and, already, it talks about how he was responsible for initial discoveries in radio, microwaves, remote control, radar, and electrical engineering. He knew so much about so many different things ... he had to have been a wizard," said Tom.

"That is a more plausible assertion than others I have heard. Some have postulated that Tesla was either a being from outer space or that he was in communication with extraterrestrials to have such a broad and advanced knowledge base," said William.

"Was he really from outer space?" asked Sera incredulously.

"I am sure that he was born here on Earth, but as to where he got his information, I have no idea. Was he extremely intuitive while following scientific method? Did he project himself into the future and then bring those ideas back? Did he have the ability to speak to spirit guides? Did he astral project to a cosmic parlor where extraterrestrials also projected to and have a chat over a spot of Earl Grey tea and walnut crescent cookies? I don't know. I do believe in what Shakespeare wrote many years ago ... there are more things in Heaven and Hell than are dreamt of in my philosophy," said William.

"Meaning you don't know but you're willing to believe anything," said Sera.

"Meaning I don't know but I am willing to *consider* anything ... even if I have never considered it before now," explained William.

William redirected the discussion back to Tom. "So, who invented the radio anyway?"

"Tesla invented the radio, but the Marconi guy made it famous and then took all the credit for it," answered Tom.

"So tell me what you have found out so far," asked William.

Tom pulled a piece of paper from his pocket and glanced at it for a moment. After refreshing his memory, he began.

"Tesla was doing experiments in eighteen ninety-three with high frequency currents and described his radio, in detail, in lectures that he gave. His ideas were then translated and sent all over the world. Two years later, Marconi shows everyone the radio he created, even though it's the same device Tesla described. When people asked about mysterious coincidence, Marconi says that he never saw any of Tesla's papers.

"If you ask me, that is pretty lame. If I copied a paper of Tesla's and handed it into my teacher as my own, I would get a big, fat F for fail. If I then told the teacher that I had never heard of Tesla, she would laugh at me. So I don't know how Marconi got away with it," said Tom.

"Well, in those days, copyright laws were not as stringently enforced as they are now. Plus, back in those days, there was no Internet, television, or telephone. Getting and sharing information was quite difficult," said William.

"Well, Tesla got smart and got a patent on his radio device. However, Marconi had been mentioned so many times with the radio that he was considered the inventor by the rest of the world," said Tom.

"What else did Tesla do?" asked Sera.

"He went out to Colorado to build a huge radio transmitter so that he could send a message from there to Paris, France. He would use that event to embarrass Marconi. But instead of sending a message, he discovered that he could send electricity without wires. The last thing I read was that Tesla did an experiment for reporters where he sent electricity over twenty-five miles to light up two hundred light bulbs and used no wires," concluded Tom.

"Very good, Tom. What do you think about what you have read so far? Do you think Tesla was a better inventor or businessman?" asked William.

"I think that he was a much better inventor. He was more interested in creating even more inventions than defending his radio work. If he had been more of a businessman, he would have gone after Marconi immediately," said Tom.

"Do you think that Edison was a better inventor or a better businessman?" asked William.

"I think that Edison was a businessman because he owned several companies and because he had lots of people working for him," answered Tom.

"I'll tell you something that your great-grandmother used to say, 'Tell me who you run with and I'll tell you what you are.' Edison had a winter home in Fort Myers, Florida, right across the street from his friend and fellow businessman, Henry Ford," said William.

"Wow! I guess Edison was a really good businessman to be in the same league as Ford," said Sera.

"It sounds like it to me," said Tom.

Chapter 18 – Touché

At that moment, the phone rang in the kitchen and William went to answer it. Judging from the discussion, Tom knew Grandpa was talking to his dad. It had only been a couple of days since Tom had spoken to his dad, but in some ways it seemed longer. The conversation went on for a few minutes before William called Tom to the phone.

Once Tom got on the phone, his dad was interested in getting the details from Tom about his river adventure. Tom told him the whole story but did not elaborate on how much he was injured. He didn't want his dad to become overprotective and bring him home. There was just too much going on here. Eventually, the discussion got around to that subject.

"Well, it sounds like you're having an entertaining time there. Do you know when you'll want to be coming home?" asked Ray.

"Uh, I don't know. I mean, I haven't thought about it really," said Tom.

"Your grandpa said something about moving a couple of trees on the property. I think that you should stay there until you get the trees moved. Don't you think that's a good idea?" suggested Ray.

"Yeah, I think that's a good idea. Grandpa could use the help, and he needs someone to keep an eye on him. You can't imagine the things he wants to do around here," said Tom loud enough for William to hear him.

William looked at him with a stern expression and waved his index finger at Tom, as if to admonish him. This quickly deteriorated into a lopsided smile and another hand gesture. William touched his thumb to his nose and waggled his four fingers in the air. Tom smiled and Sera loudly snorted. They both looked at Sera in amusement. She immediately blushed and hid behind a pillow.

"Yeah, my dad's got a pretty good imagination. Keep him out of trouble and help him out as much as you can. Give us a call next weekend or whenever you want. Just keep us informed on how it's going, OK?" said Ray.

"Sure, Dad, it's no problem. I'll give you a call next weekend," said Tom.

After they said their goodbyes, Ray hung up the phone, which was sitting on the nightstand next to his bed, and looked over at Karen, who stood in the doorway to their bedroom.

"Our boy is doing some growing up and that's for sure," said Ray.

"So he's doing OK? I thought I overheard that he was hurt?" asked Karen.

"He's in good hands, sweetheart. Dad may let him get some bumps and bruises, but he won't let him get injured. It took me a while to understand that. Sometimes a little bit of hurt is just what you need to gain some wisdom. Based upon what Dad said and what Tom didn't say, I think the two of them are doing very well," said Ray.

"I guess that's true. I thought for sure he would want to be home with his computer by now," said Karen.

Ray stood up, gave his wife a hug and said, "A computer game will never match up to life ... there are a lot more variables."

Tom came back from the kitchen and limped to the couch, where he plopped down and sighed, "OK. I told Dad that I haven't died yet and that I should hang out here a bit longer."

"Cool," said Sera, "I just talked to my parents on William's cell phone and they said I could spend the night. This is much more interesting than being home and surfing the Internet."

"Well then, I guess now is the time to give you a little zap," said William.

"What do you mean by a little zap? Do you have a Tesla ray gun under the couch or something?" laughed Tom.

"No, I have something a bit more interesting than that," said William.

William sat down next to Tom on the couch. He had Tom lie back on the couch and put his sore ankle on his lap. William then gently placed his hands on Tom's sore ankle and closed his eyes.

"What are you doing?" asked Tom.

"It looks like he's praying," said Sera.

"I am trying to concentrate. Tom, tell Sera what you feel until I open my eyes again," said William.

Tom continued to lay back and wait for something to happen although he had no idea where he should focus his attention. He looked over to Sera, who was looking back at him, and shrugged his shoulders. He opened his mouth to say something to Sera but stopped with his mouth open. He closed his mouth and his eyes widened. He was looking as though he heard a really high-pitched noise. To complete the image, he then cocked his head to the left.

"What's going on?" asked Sera excitedly.

"It's weird. It feels like his hands are getting hot," said Tom.

Sera immediately got up and walked over to William. She very gently put her finger next to William's hand where it touched Tom's ankle.

"It does feel warm," said Sera, smiling as if she had just witnessed a magic trick.

Sera sat down on the floor at William's feet, curled her dark hair behind her ears and watched intently. William continued to sit quietly and hold his hands around Tom's ankle. Tom continued to focus on the steady increase of heat radiating around his ankle. At one point, he wondered if his grandpa had slipped a hot pack under his hands when he wasn't looking. But he knew better than that.

After about ten minutes, Tom felt the heat subsiding. William took a couple of deep breaths and then opened his eyes and smiled.

"OK, what the heck was that?!" asked Tom excitedly.

"That was reiki," said William.

"OK, what the heck is reiki?!" asked Tom again.

"Remember that picture in the hall of the monks in their red and gold robes?" asked William.

"Yeah, it's the one with the bowls sitting in front of them," said Tom.

"Well, those guys are Buddhist monks; reiki is a Buddhist healing technique made popular in Japan," said William.

"I think that it's time for William to give *us* a report," said Sera, smiling.

"I think Sera has an outstanding idea," said Tom.

"I think you guys are ganging up on me," said William with a grin.

William looked to his right and to his left as two pair of amused and curious eyes looked back at him. He took a deep breath and rubbed his hands together as if they were cold. Once he was settled, he began.

"When you guys are feeling bad, does your mom or dad give you a hug?" asked William.

"Yes," answered Sera and Tom in unison.

"When a small child has a small hurt, a boo-boo, have you ever seen them go to their mommy and have it kissed?" asked William.

Both Sera and Tom nodded in the affirmative.

"Some would say that these are outward signs of concern and affection. However, beyond the outward signs, there are a number of physiological responses too. These activities lower blood pressure, pulse rate, increase the flow of endorphins, and can decrease the amount of pain that people say they feel.

"Reiki acknowledges this same effect, but with more of an Eastern philosophy. Reiki is a way for chi, also known as universal life force or universal energy, to be transmitted through the reiki practitioner and into the person who needs it. As a result of this conduction of energy, reiki can restore balance to systems within the body. This applies to physical, mental, emotional, and/or spiritual, depending upon the recipient's needs."

"So you just sent energy into his body?" asked Sera.

"It would be more accurate to say that I am a conduit of energy. Think of the Universe being the battery charger, I am the cables, and Tom is the depleted battery," said William.

"So it's a lot like our saltwater experiment, except you are the saltwater and I'm the light bulb. Do your hands heat up like that all the time?" asked Tom.

William was enormously pleased at the association Tom had made but kept it to himself. Little Eagle was right about Tom; Little Eagle was nearly always right. Still, William needed to give an answer.

"No, not always. Most times they heat up less than what they just did. Sometimes I can't tell if they are heating up or not. Usually the person I am helping tells me," replied William.

"How did you learn about reiki? Did you live in ... in whatever country Buddhists live in?" asked Sera.

"Actually, Buddhism is a philosophy, so it is not restricted to any one country. Of course, the Chinese government would say they are restricted from their country. Anyway, I did not learn it from a Buddhist. I learned it at a seminar of complementary and alternative medicine given by a Benedictine monk. The laying on of hands for healing energy goes back a way in the Judeo-Christian tradition too," replied William.

"Where can I go to learn something like that?" asked Tom.

"Well, you need to find someone who believes that you are ready to learn such things. That someone also needs to be a reiki master. Since you happen to be looking at a reiki master at this moment, you need only demonstrate that you are ready for learning such things," said William.

"When will that be?" asked Tom.

"Soon. Not today, but soon," said William.

"So is reiki from Buddhists or from that other group you mentioned?" asked Sera.

"Actually, reiki is a Japanese word. The concept of reiki was rediscovered by Mikao Usui, a Japanese Buddhist, who was interested in healing. He rediscovered the concept of reiki when he studied ancient texts written in Sanskrit but stored in a Buddhist temple. Once he learned it, he traveled around, healing and teaching as he went. Reiki made it from Japan to Hawaii and to the rest of the United States," said William.

"I want to learn reiki too. My mom was in a car accident and she always has back pain and migraines," said Sera.

"I did not know that. Tell you what, Sera, I will send some reiki to your mom tonight. When you talk to her tomorrow, ask how she is feeling," said William.

"So can we have a reiki class tomorrow?" asked Tom.

"No, I have plans for you tomorrow that will be just as beneficial. In fact, it will help you in every area of your life. You will be more understanding of people, you will have an easier time in school, and you will have ability to bring into your life the things you desire," said William with a smile.

"What is it, Grandpa?" asked Tom.

"It is the same thing I used the day I picked that word out of the air," said William.

With that comment, William stood up, excused himself, and left the room heading down the hallway.

Sera was not fully aware of the incident where William picked the word *waddle* out of thin air. Without telling her about the relationship of the word and how he was mistreated at school, Tom told her the story. She shook her head in disbelief. On one hand, William seemed so normal. On the other hand, he seemed so different because of all these different things he could do. Then again, it wasn't as though he was truly unique because he was doing things that other people had done before him. That was a question that she would have to get answered. How does he do it?

William returned and told them that he had made sure that the bedroom at the end of the hall was ready for her. He reminded her where the bathroom was and announced that he was going to bed. As he headed toward his bedroom, Sera asked him a question.

"William, you know all these different types of unique or uncommon information. I know that you aren't a magician because they use illusions. What would you call yourself?"

William stood in the doorway of his bedroom for a moment. He then leaned against the frame for support, as if the question bore a weight that he was not expecting. In that moment, both Tom and Sera were startled to see him so weakened.

"It seems that the older I get, the more complicated that question becomes to answer ... at least in a manner that's satisfactory to me," said William. After a sigh, William tried to answer Sera's question.

"As soon as you label a thing, you limit a thing. Yet to be unlabeled is to be either unknown or not understood."

William sighed and spoke again, "I am a Christian, a Buddhist, a Spiritualist, a Skeptic, a Gnostic, a visionary, a teacher, a businessman, a carpenter, an energetic healer, a dog lover, a grandfather, an environmentalist, and a herbalist, and that was just for today. Tomorrow is another day."

"Dad says you are a 'jack of all trades' ... whatever that means," said Tom.

"Can you sum all of that up into something easier to understand?" asked Sera.

"To keep it simple, I am an alchemist. I draw from the elements around me, and I create my reality. That will have to do for now," said William.

"I thought those guys were imaginary or magicians from the olden days? " asked Tom.

"Yeah, weren't those the guys who tried to turn stone into gold?" asked Sera.

William had a quick flash of a smile that seemed more whimsical than humorous before he replied.

"Not all stones are made of stone. Not all gold is made of gold."

William moved into his room and closed his door. Sera and Tom looked at each other with mutual degrees of curiosity. Why did William find it so hard to define himself? That answer would have to wait for now.

Chapter 19 – Movie Theater

The next day began with an early morning of coffee making and playing with the dogs. William watched from the porch as Sid, Quan, Sera, and Tom were playing catch with a rather tired-looking tennis ball. The early morning wake-up programming had worked for Sera. She told herself to wake up at 6:55 and repeated the number several times before falling asleep. That morning she opened her eyes and the clock showed 6:54. She smiled brightly and began her day by waking up Tom. Tom had fallen asleep immediately and had not done the programming.

William smiled over his cup of Jamaican Blue. It was hard to tell who was keeping away from who as Sid would chase down the ball and then sit down with it until someone got close. Then, he would bolt away for about ten seconds only to lie down again. Quan, finally, would chase after Sid and then he'd drop the ball to escape.

Eventually, William called them in for something to eat. They sat around the table, eating and laughing at how the dogs chased the ball, each other and them. After breakfast, William asked Tom to take a couple more of the herbal pills and sit down and relax while he gave him another reiki session. His ankle was giving him a little aggravation, especially since he had been out playing with the dogs. However, after the reiki session, Tom felt no pain.

With necessities out of the way, William invited them both down to the office/classroom again. They noticed that William was not as talkative today as he had been in the past. They thought that maybe this was carried over from last night, but the real reason became clear once they were in the classroom and settled. William looked at them both with a seriousness that neither of them had seen before today.

"My friends, today is a very significant day for both of you. I am going to teach you a technique of mind control that not very many people know and yet everyone should practice. After today, things will never be the same. By seeing the world from a different perspective, you will see possibilities that you have never seen before. Are you ready to continue?" asked William.

With wide eyes, both Tom and Sera nodded that they were ready.

"There will be no experiment in the barn today because what I have planned for class will be a life-changing event for everyone here. Today, we will become peers in potential. I will have the benefits and difficulties that go along with advanced chronological age. You will have the benefits and difficulties of youth and naiveté. If we can stay in touch, we can do some amazing things together. At the same time, you will have to learn and discover many things on your own. The act of discovery is, itself, a great teacher."

"Maybe that is why I dreamt of being in the barn, but it was too dark to see anything in there," said Tom.

"The first thing I want to do," said William, "is to install your imaginary movie screen. I want you to become relaxed and then follow my direction as I am speaking. What we will do is imagine a movie theater in your head. It will be a screen as big or as small as you want it to be. It will have more than movies though. Anything you may want to know or ask the Universe for can be seen here. I guess it will be a combination of a movie theater screen and computer screen. Follow me so far?"

"Can it be a stage?" asked Sera.

"I would prefer that it not be. When seeking answers, you will sometimes find them unpleasant. It would be better to see things from a distant perspective as opposed to being right in the middle of them," said William.

William walked over to the doorway and dimmed the lights to almost complete darkness. He then started a tape playing that had both a humming sound and the sound of ocean waves meeting the beach. As soon as Tom and Sera got comfortable, William began.

"We will be building a screen in your mind for you to access information as you need it. This screen will be a way for you to ask the Universe for information, to seek solutions to problems, or just to relax. Now, I want you to breathe deeply and slowly. Feel your body relaxing. Your mental movie screen is a tool for your mind to allow the positive changes you desire to appear in your life.

"Keep taking deep breaths. Fill your belly and then your lungs. Hold it for a second and then exhale. After you do that, I want you to feel your eyelids getting heavy. Continue by feeling your shoulders relaxing and breathing deeply. As your breathing deepens, it slows. Your mind becomes quiet and more peaceful."

192

William paused for a few seconds for everything to sink in and allow them to relax. He did not want them to fall asleep though, so he continued before the snoring started.

"As you continue relaxing your body and mind, imagine that you are going down in an elevator. See the floors going by. Count them: ten, nine, eight, seven. You are becoming more physically relaxed and mentally alert. Six, five, four. Feel all tension leave your body. Three, two, one. You are now very relaxed and yet mentally alert. At any time during this exercise, you may open your eyes, feel completely awake, relaxed, and ready to attend to any task necessary. Also, you may accept or reject anything that I say.

"Imagine you are in a movie theater. You are seated in the most comfortable of chairs and are relaxed. This is your theater so you can imagine whatever colors, seats, speakers, and flooring that you want. In this room, your chair is facing a screen. It is as big or as small as you want it to be. Imagine this screen a good distance away. You can see everything clearly on this screen without any strain or discomfort.

"When you are in your theater, you are relaxed and functioning in a level of the brain called alpha. It is a place where you can be relaxed and restful, yet still aware. When you are in this place, you will attract increased health, prosperity, and happiness to your life. The more you are in this place, you will find it easier to achieve and maintain alpha level with your mind. Your senses and abilities will improve every time you function at this level with your mind."

Again, William paused to allow the information to sink in and to take a sip of water. After a moment, he continued.

"We have all heard of geniuses: Albert Einstein, Nikola Tesla, Leonardo Da Vinci, Carl Sagan. What these men had in common was that they used their brains a bit differently than other people do. With your mental movie screen, you are using your brain a bit differently than other people do. With your increasing mental capabilities, comes responsibility. If you attempt to use your increased mental abilities for any other purpose than for the overall good of humanity, you will be unable to function at this level with your mind.

"The first thing I want you to do is look at the screen and see yourself. As you see yourself on the screen, see yourself looking happy, confident, intelligent, and compassionate. See yourself getting good grades on your homework. See yourself passing tests with ease. It feels so good for all of these things to be happening.

"Now imagine someone in your family. Does this person have a mental or physical problem? If so, see the person on the screen. See the person being washed over in a rainbow of colors. Now see this person feeling better and better. See this person smiling and happy.

"This movie theater is always available to you and can change its shape or form to serve you. Your trigger for accessing this theater is to imagine your elevator and counting the floors from ten to one. This is your movie theater. You may enter and leave as you please.

"Now, imagine the lights getting brighter and the movie ending. Imagine that you are getting up and stretching. Imagine walking out of the theater and into the elevator. You are going to come back now and on the count of ten, you will be wide awake, refreshed, and ready for any new experiences that may come your way. One, two, three. Feel yourself becoming more aware. Four, five six. Feeling better than before. Seven, eight, nine, ten. You are now wide awake and refreshed."

William returned to the light switch and gradually brought the lights back to normal brightness. He turned to see two pairs of blinking eyes staring at him. Smiling, but unsure of any change, they looked at him, then at each other.

"Now, you may wonder if any of this means anything at all, really. I will tell you that it means whatever you want it to mean. If you think this was just a fun little experiment and then you forget about it, then that's all it will be. However, if you feel as though something important and real happened, then try this ... sometime today, go back to your movie theater and try it again. Sera, see your mom feeling better. Tom, see your ankle feeling better," said William.

"What's really weird is that I feel as if I've had another night's sleep since we have been sitting here," said Tom.

"Me too. How long have we been down here?" asked Sera.

"About an hour," said William.

Amazement was seen on both of their faces. and they laughed. It had seemed like much longer.

"OK, Sera, you had best be heading for home before your parents become too worried," said William.

"Yeah, they have to let you come back tomorrow, you know," said Tom smiling.

"All right then," said Sera with an artificial pout on her face.

After Sera had gone, Tom told his grandpa that while he was in the theater, he thought he heard classical guitar music. William just smiled. He also often heard guitar music while in an alpha state.

As Sera returned home, she was anxious to share what she had learned. She was also eager to see how her mother was feeling after the long distance reiki healing William had performed. She could just see her parent's faces when she talked about reiki, astral projection, Tesla. The more she thought about it, the more she had second thoughts. By the time she got home, Sera thought that she would tell them about reiki first. If that went over well, then she would tell them more. She didn't want her parents to freak out and then not let her go over to William's house any more.

While sitting in the classroom, William gave Tom another reiki treatment. This time William's hands did not seem as hot. However, Tom's ankle was not hurting like the night before and he had not been on it during the whole class. Once the reiki treatment was over, William had Tom stay in the library while he went out to the barn and handled a few loose ends with work. He also had another experiment that he wanted to set up.

Sera came home and saw her mom first. Elena was doing laundry at the time and had the stereo up loud. Since she could not hear her, Sera crept into the house, quietly walked into the laundry room and shouted, "¡Hola!"

Elena had an armful of socks in her arms when she heard Sera. She screamed and threw the socks in such a way that it looked like a fluffy fireworks display.

"¡Madre de Diós! ¿Sera estás loca? Tu realmente me asustó!"

Laughing, Sera gave her mom a quick kiss on the cheek and then skipped into the kitchen to see if there was anything good in there for snacking. Elena tried to swat Sera on the butt playfully, but missed. Within a few moments, Elena came into the kitchen too.

"Pues, ¿cómo era la noche pasada?"

"It was great! We stayed up and told stories, we had snacks, we played with the dogs, and William taught Tom and I about Buddhists," said Sera.

Elena raised an eyebrow, but said nothing.

"¿Cómo está Tom? ¿Se siente mejor? ¿Qué hizo anoche?"

"Tom is feeling better. He is walking around with a limp but William got him feeling better. I really didn't do too much. I just kept Tom company for a while in the library. William has him working on a project, so he was doing a lot of reading," said Sera.

While they were talking, Sera noticed that her mother was in a constant state of motion. She was cleaning the countertop, putting a couple of dishes into the dishwasher, or straightening the magnets on the refrigerator. This was unlike her to be so energetic.

"Mom, how are you feeling today?" asked Sera.

"I'm fine. Why do you ask?" asked Elena.

"I'm noticing that you are full of energy today. I thought that you were nervous or something," said Sera.

"Well, I feel pretty good today because my back doesn't hurt like it normally does," said Elena.

"Hmm," replied Sera.

She made a mental note to tell Tom and William that the distance reiki treatment had an obvious effect on her mom. Unfortunately, circumstances would unfold that would prevent that from happening.

Chapter 20 – Foreshadowing

Tom continued reading about Tesla while his grandpa worked out in the garage. He was excited and curious at the same time when he read about Tesla. Tesla had been so prolific in his stream of inventions. At the same time, Tesla was rarely mentioned in any science or history book he ever read in school. Every time he read about them, Tom was fascinated by the experiments where Tesla generated electricity. Tom decided that he should read everything that he could on Tesla.

Later, William and Tom had dinner and shared their thoughts on why Tesla was not more famous or, at least, recognized. When Tom announced that he wanted to read more things about Tesla, William was quietly excited. Tesla had been a hero of William's since his adolescence, and he was glad to share his passion with another. William told Tom that he would have to go into town tomorrow to pick up a few things and to finalize the process for the new customer at work. As the night drew to a close, William made sure that his friends Sid and Quan were fed, gave Tom a little reiki boost, and then went to bed.

Somewhere along the path of Life, nearly everyone has realized that Life is what happens while you are busy making plans, and both Tom and William were no exception. William found that the demands created by his new contract were more than anticipated, so he was at the factory almost every day the following week. Tom was getting around OK, but still had a twinge here and there that told him not to push his luck. During this time, he had some unusual dreams. However, soon after awakening, he would be unable to recall what happened. It was as though he was learning something that could only be taught while he was asleep.

Rather than wasting his time napping, as he had done before he came to stay with his grandpa, Tom was using the time he had and was practicing going into his mental theater. At first, he had problems relaxing his mind without falling asleep. However, with a little practice, Tom was able to go to his theater and watch his ankle get better. A couple of days later, he decided to see himself getting really good grades at school and finding money. He was not completely sure if it was going to work or not. After about three days, his ankle was feeling as good as new, but he was not sure if his body or his mind was the reason. Maybe it was both.

Sitting around was not very interesting without either TV or the Internet as distractions, so as soon as he was able, Tom was taking the Jeep out to the trees. Of course, Quan was always quick to follow. On his first time back out there, Tom took his time. The thought of hurting his ankle kept his pace at a manageable level. However, the next day he was digging away just as before he was hurt. He actually liked being outside and working with his hands. Tom thought that it was ironic that he enjoyed the same things that his father and brother did. He had never wanted to participate with them before because Mark always ended up being pushy and acting superior. That day, Tom decided that he would add another movie into the theater. Mark was going to treat him better and he was not going to be as upset at the things Mark said.

As the days continued, William would still be home for dinner each evening, and he and Tom would tell each other stories of how the day had gone for each of them. William was happy to get all of the loose ends tied up with his new client and was proud of Tom for taking the initiative to go out to the trees again. Tom was glad for his grandpa's support. Unexpectedly, Tom was happy to hear his grandpa talk about work. It was comforting to hear stories about normal day-to-day activities. After many days of talking about different nationalities, philosophies, dream interpretation, astral projection, and such, it was nice just to have a discussion that didn't stretch your beliefs. Maybe it was because the normal, down-to-earth discussions reminded him of home.

After being there a month, Tom decided that he should be going home soon. It was cool hanging out with Grandpa and learning all of this neat stuff, but the world of familiar things still called to him. He missed his TV and his video games. He missed his mom's cooking and the restaurant in his town that had his favorite—cheeseburgers and pizza. Tom was convinced that as soon as the trees were moved, he would go back home.

The extra work Tom had put into the tree project paid off. Once William was able to stay home again, the two of them made short work of the project. With the winch on the front of the Jeep, they were able to pull out each of the trees and almost the entire root ball. Once the root ball was covered with the burlap material, it was rolled onto a makeshift sled William had attached to the back of the Jeep. It took them three days to uproot, tie up, and relocate the trees, but they managed it with considerable effort. The third night they had a big dinner to celebrate. William had made a large rack of barbecued ribs and a side dish made from apples and potatoes called Heaven and Earth. Freshly made brownies were the perfect ending to a perfect meal.

That night, Tom thought about how different life at home would be after his wizard/alchemist apprenticeship over the past two months. He was thinking about school when he drifted off to sleep.

Tom was walking down the hallway of a school. He knew it was a school because of the doors and lockers, but he also knew that it was not his school. He was walking down a hallway, looking at the display cases, when he heard a familiar voice.

"Hi, there," said Little Eagle. It was Little Eagle, but he was dressed as though he were a modern-day student.

"Hi, there, yourself. Where the heck have you been?" asked Tom.

"I have been keeping an eye on you, that's where I have been. Why are you leaving William's house today?" asked Little Eagle.

"I figured that it was time to get back home ... to get back to familiar things ... to see if this mental imagery stuff really works," said Tom.

"Oh, that's done easily enough. When you wake up tomorrow, you'll have your answer," said Little Eagle with certainty.

Little Eagle was so confident that Tom did not even think to debate him on the issue. He instead asked, "Why do we even go to school?"

"Life is a school ... a school that never closes. The school that you are thinking of is more like a factory. Every child gets approximately the same education because there is no time or money for deviation," said Little Eagle.

"I know what you mean now. There's so much more out there than I ever knew. If it weren't for Grandpa teaching me to question the answers I have been given, I would be missing out on a lot," said Tom.

"More than that, Tom. Learning to think for yourself instead of believing what you are told by an authority figure will make you wise, intelligent, and, in some places, dangerous. The truth can be both sword and shield. Know that there are those who would prefer you were unarmed," said Little Eagle with great intensity.

"What do you know that you are not telling me?" asked Tom with a bit of worry.

"I know that you are on the edge of some exciting times. You will have three homecomings in short succession. Soon thereafter, you will be challenged. It is through challenges that you grow stronger in ability and belief. Once through any challenge, you will be rewarded in numerous ways," said Little Eagle.

"Three homecomings? Challenges? The last time we talked like this, you were telling me about self-reliance and then I nearly drowned!" exclaimed Tom.

"Yes, this is true. But you did not drown. You also have a different perspective of reality now, don't you? You have become more of the world—not just in it," said Little Eagle.

"Any other cryptic pieces of advice that you would like to give me?" asked Tom.

"Use the rosewood-colored paint," said Little Eagle with a mischievous smile.

At that moment, the school bell rang and kids flooded the hall. As kids whisked by going to class or to their lockers, Little Eagle was enveloped by them and disappeared. As Tom watched the kids go by, one stuck out for obvious reasons. He was about Tom's age but looked older. He was wearing black from head to foot. The long overcoat covered almost all of him except for the cuff on his pant and the boots that stuck out from underneath. The two of them locked their gaze upon each other. Tom could not decide if he was going to go up to him and say something. Suddenly, the kid screamed at him.

"Stay away from me! I'm not going to tell you!"

It scared Tom so badly that he woke up with a start and looked about the bedroom to see if there was a person in the room. As he looked around, he realized that it was just a dream and that it was late in the morning. Tom got dressed and hurried out to the kitchen where his grandpa was on the phone.

"Here he is now, so let me ask him," said William.

"Felipe is on the phone and wants to know if you would like to come over and help him paint his house. He said that he would pay you pretty well for helping him out."

"Yeah, sure! After all the great things he's done for me. Heck, it would be the least I could do," said Tom.

After some breakfast, William took Tom over to the Lopez place. It was the first time he got a good look at it. It was a beautiful A-frame log cabin, onto which Felipe had added a large room and a workshop. Elena had planted flowers all around the cabin and along side the pathway that led to the front. In the daylight, you could see that it could really benefit from a coat of paint. When they arrived, they saw Felipe with two buckets of paint and two brushes. He was trying to decide between a gray and a brown with reddish overtones.

"So, what do you think?" asked Felipe.

"I think you should go with the rosewood color," said Tom.

"How did you know that the color is called Rosewood?" said Felipe.

"Just psychic, I guess," said Tom with a smile similar to William's.

"Why do you think that this is the color to use?" asked Felipe.

"Well, it's very similar to what is on there now. It won't show up if you happen to miss a spot, and you should be able to get away with just one coat," replied Tom.

"Brilliant, just brilliant. I'll call Elena while she and Sera are out shopping and tell her to pick up another five gallons of this color so we can get started," said Felipe.

"Well, I guess I will check in at work to make sure things are going well. Tom, would I be correct in assuming that you will not be going home this evening?" asked William.

"Nope, I want to stay until we finish the paint job here," said Tom.

"All right then, I will be back around dinner time to pick you up. Felipe, is that all right with you?"

"Sí, está muy bien."

"Bien. Tom, I'll see you later," said William as he put the Jeep in gear and headed to the factory.

Chapter 21 – Auf Wiedersehen

The work wasn't easy. Nearly the entire exterior needed to be scrubbed with a wire brush so that the paint would stick properly. While they scrubbed, Tom learned that the Lopez family was selling the house because they had to move. As much as he didn't want to, Felipe had to move his family to someplace closer to a city. The company he worked for currently was laying off workers, and he would be one of them. He had a month to find a job and, living out here, he was very far from any decent opportunities.

Tom was surprised to hear this. He didn't want them to move because he liked to know that Sera was here. Every time he visited his grandpa, he could visit with Sera. That gave him a feeling of comfort and happiness. His sudden realization of this fact was his second surprise. Did this mean that he wanted Sera to be his girlfriend? *Does Sera like me that way?* he thought. Briefly, he imagined what it would be like for them to be going out together. Suddenly wondering if Felipe could read his mind, Tom quickly looked at him. But Felipe was just scrubbing away. Feeling a bit embarrassed, surprised, and confused, Tom got lost in his thoughts by doing some scrubbing of his own.

The hours upon hours spent digging up and transplanting trees had made their mark on Tom. Tom had lost the pudginess that had plagued him in his first year of high school. The change of diet, away from hamburgers and pizza, helped quite a bit too. Because of this, Tom looked more tan and lean than he ever had. His increased stamina was obvious too. He took the effort needed to scrub away the old paint in stride. Both Tom and Felipe took occasional breaks to have some water and to rest a bit, but Tom kept pace with Felipe the entire day.

Once the sun started to hang low in the sky, Tom started to feel a bit tired. He had not eaten lunch because the work in the hot sun had taken away his appetite. Now that things were slowing down for the day, he was ready to reconsider. As if on cue, his stomach rumbling for something to eat coincided with William pulling up to retrieve Tom. William hopped out and dropped the tailgate to reveal an electric air compressor and a paint gun. Between the barn and the garage, it seemed that William had a tool or toy for almost any occasion.

"It may be a bit late for this, but as I was straightening up things in the garage, I found this power paint gun. If you still need it, as it appears you do, I am willing to lend it to you," said William.

"Additional help is never late when there's still work to be done," said Felipe.

Tom helped William unload the paint sprayer and listened to him explain how to use it to both he and Felipe. Somewhat disappointed that he did not get to see Sera, Tom hopped into the Jeep while William said goodbye to Felipe.

"Wait! Tom! You forgot something," said Felipe.

Felipe walked up to the car door and handed Tom a fifty-dollar bill. Tom's eyes got really big. Finally, he found his voice.

"I can't take this. I'm helping you paint because you were so good to me when I showed up in your backyard," said Tom.

"Trust me, for the work that you did, you were worth every penny. Anyway, I would have to have had to pay complete strangers even more money to do this work. This way, I am saving a bit of money and I know the money I give is going to an honorable person," said Felipe.

Tom was speechless. He wanted to cry with joy; the compliment he had just received felt like a thousand dollars. Suddenly, he realized that his discussion with Little Eagle had come true. Tom had visualized that he would find some money and Little Eagle said that today he would have his answer. Stunned, he could only look at Felipe.

"The eyes say it all, amigo," said Felipe.

He gave a fraternal pat to Tom's shoulder and headed back to the house. Tom looked over at William, who was now behind the wheel of the Jeep. He just raised his eyebrows, smiled, and then headed for home. Sometimes, Tom thought, words are not enough to express the power of emotions.

Dinner was spent as most dinners were. There was not much discussion of inventors or metaphysics. The discussion was mostly about day-to-day activities. In the back of Tom's mind, though, was the eventuality of his departure. He thought that it was sort of ironic that he arrived here and really didn't want to stay as long as he did and now he was leaving and really didn't want to go.

After dinner was finished, Tom volunteered to feed the dogs. William agreed, and while Tom was tapping on Sid and Quan, William called his son and told him that Tom would be returning in the next day or two. Ray thought that it was a good idea since school would be starting in the next couple of weeks.

When Tom came back upstairs, he noticed that William had brought a chair from another room and placed it next to the couch. William was searching for a particular CD as Tom flopped onto the couch.

"So, do I correctly sense another reiki treatment coming on?" asked Tom.

"Not completely ... reiki will be involved, but it will not be the only thing I will be doing. Go ahead and stretch out on the couch. Until now, I have only focused reiki on your ankle. Tonight will be a full reiki treatment," said William.

The stereo began to play music recorded by Tibetan Buddhist monks using metal bowls. It was both striking and soothing to Tom. William sat in the chair and proceeded to put his hands on the top of Tom's head. His hands hovered, ever so slightly, above his head but never touched. He continued by placing his hands over Tom's forehead, eyes, throat, heart, stomach, bladder, hips, knees, ankles, and the soles of his feet. At each location, William hovered a few minutes, but never lingered for quite the same amount of time.

After several minutes, Tom was breathing deep and had nearly drifted to sleep. William was hoping for just that thing. He wanted to help Tom with more programming. There was no need to count backwards, as Tom was already very relaxed. William started at the elevator and got Tom to his mental movie theater.

William asked Tom to continue doing what he had been doing since he had first arrived. Keep an open mind. Question the answers. Spend less time looking at what people do and think about why they do it. Remember that things are different now. Remember that you are different now. Remember that you have something in common with the greatest minds of all time. This continued until William could think of no more to say. He kissed Tom on the forehead and left him to sleep on the couch.

Right after breakfast the next day, Tom was over at the Lopez house and was eager to tell Sera about the discussion he had with Little Eagle in his theater. He wanted to tell her about how sorry he was that they were moving. He wanted to tell her that he cared for her ... but he also knew that he wouldn't. He was sure that if he told her that he liked her, trouble would soon follow. She would probably whap him upside his head and tell him to get over it. Still, he had things to tell her.

Unfortunately, when he arrived, she was gone with Elena again. They were driving to two different cities that Felipe thought were good places and were looking for nice apartments that they could live in for a while. Again, they would be gone all day. It was really frustrating for Tom to have this newly gained information and not be able to share it with someone who he cared about and who cared about these types of things.

Felipe had gotten an early start too. He had been scraping for almost two hours before Tom got there. Most of the house was ready for painting, so Felipe took a break from scraping. Together, they got the painting rig set up and working. After Felipe had a turn, Tom took over and finished what Felipe left behind. Tom's hands were a bit sore from yesterday, but the calluses and muscles he had developed from moving a couple of trees were now his hard-won friends. By the time they stopped for a late lunch, Tom was done. Over a couple of sandwiches, they chatted.

"You are a good worker, Tom. You must come from good stock," said Felipe.

"Good stock? Oh, good genes. I guess so. My dad loves to work with his hands and he likes being outside. He's a fireman. Mom says he's part man and part bear. My brother is kind of like that too. He likes to be outside, but it's usually when there is someone there he can either impress or boss around," said Tom.

"Remember, the ones who need to impress are usually the ones who feel they are lacking something. Also remember that there is a difference between being bossy and being the boss," said Felipe.

"Well, Mark has the bossy thing down pretty good," said Tom with a grin. "But speaking of bosses, are you looking to be a boss or a manager somewhere?"

"The company I work for is offering placement assistance to its full-time employees. Unfortunately, I am a contractor and as such, I will not get that assistance. So, I need to find my own job, find a place to live, and get this place sold, all at the same time. I'll take whatever job I can find," said Felipe.

"So, are you still going to repair computers or do something else?" asked Tom.

"Well, I grew up on a farm and taught myself how to use computers. Then I taught myself how to repair them. Recently, I have been teaching myself how to network them wirelessly. That's why I have all of those computers and the router in my front room. However, without a document showing my qualifications, I am at a disadvantage," said Felipe.

The rest of the day went pretty quick. The paint sprayer made the process much easier and quicker. They had the place painted and cleaned up by the time William showed up. He got out of the Jeep and applauded their efforts. Felipe thanked William for the use of the sprayer and helped Tom load it up. At that moment, Felipe's cell phone rang.

"This is the realtor who is listing the house for sale. I will have to talk to you later," said Felipe.

"OK ... I will be going home tomorrow so 'later' won't be real soon," said Tom.

Felipe took the phone and slipped it into his shirt pocket. He looked at Tom for a couple of seconds as if to memorize his face.

"Well, I will sure miss you. You have been a great help to me and a good friend to my daughter. Every young man should be like you," said Felipe, who then held out his hand.

Tom and Felipe shook hands, more like parting friends than friendly neighbors. He handed Tom his business card and pointed to the cell phone number. Tom nodded his head that he understood; he could call whenever he wanted. Felipe was the first adult friend he had ever had outside of his family. Tom thought that it was pretty cool. In fact, he felt a little choked up. Little Eagle was right; the world was a different place now.

Chapter 22 – Revelations

Later that evening, William and Tom had unloaded the Jeep, fed the dogs, and eaten dinner, and they were relaxing in the solarium while the last pink and purple hues of sunset faded away. They had gone through the motions of the evening as though it was any other day. It wasn't though ... it was the last day. William had seen the turmoil on his grandson's young face ever since they came home, but he decided that Tom needed to wrestle with it on his own for a little while. Now that dinner was over, it was time to address the subject.

"Well?" asked William.

"Well what?" asked Tom.

An inquisitive look was William's only reply. Tom decided that this was his cue to speak his mind. He did.

"Grandpa, this summer has been fantastic. It kept changing almost every day with reading, discovery, experiments ... it has been more than I could have ever imagined. I have learned so much about you, me, life ... I have learned so much about the world that I would not have learned anywhere else. Part of me wants to leave so that I can try out the things I have learned. But part of me wants to stay because I want to learn more," said Tom.

"Tom, it has meant so much to me to have you come and stay with me. You have renewed my hopes in the future with your eagerness to learn and your ability to set aside preconceived notions long enough to see if a new idea might work out better. You are smart, kind, funny, and eager to learn, and your ability to ask pertinent questions is amazing. You don't even realize how amazing you truly are … and that is just one of your strengths.

"You are going to leave this Shangri-La and go back to the real world where people have not changed. They will still play their familiar roles and will expect you to play yours. Do not … do not … do not. Play this new role that you have just created. A man, much wiser than I, said the world is a stage and we are the players. This role you have created was always there inside of you. You just needed a different stage to bring it out. When you return, it will be easier to return to your former role. Resist it with all your might, for the person you have become is what most aspire to become. Be an example to others so that, perhaps, they will challenge their roles too. Once you start living the change you want, change will occur.

"Finally, you need to know you are welcome here at any time. I mean any time you want. Two days, two weeks, two years, two o'clock in the morning … you are welcome. My garage is never locked, so even if I am not home, you are welcome to come in that way. You might have to throw Sid and Quan some lunch meat, but come in and be at peace. Think of this place as your home away from home. When things are difficult or challenging for you, call me and I will do what I can. If you need reiki, a good plate of hummus, or a reality check for anything going on in your life, this is the place."

Tom got up off the couch, walked over to his grandpa's chair, and gave him a hug.

"I love you, Grandpa. Most kids just get money from their grandparents. You gave me a new way to look at the world."

Each of them took strength and comfort from their tearful embrace. In this moment, a lifelong partnership was forged that would change the way many people looked at Life. This partnership would lead to books, speeches, tours around the country, and, eventually, an International Peace Conference where both would be keynote speakers. These, and many more fascinating things, were in store for them. For now, a grandfather and grandson hugged and hoped for the best.

Sleep that night was hard to come by for both of them. Both were a bit anxious about the future and what it would hold for each of them now. It was Tom who would be the last to fall asleep. What a reward Tom got, once he was asleep! As soon as he drifted off, Little Eagle was waiting for him.

"It's about time you got here!" exclaimed Little Eagle.

"Sorry about that. Sometimes it's hard for me to turn off the thoughts in my head and get to sleep," said Tom.

"Well, I'm glad that you finally got here. I have something that I want to tell you. I have been waiting for the right time and for the right level for you to know this," said Little Eagle.

"The right level?" asked Tom.

"Yes, I want your higher self to know something. You will eventually know it in your waking mind, when it is time. For the time being, listen," said Little Eagle.

217

"OK," said Tom, and he patiently waited.

Little Eagle waved his hand and a miniature tree appeared in the air. It had a golden hue and was almost three feet tall. The top of the tree was blurry, much like a picture out of focus. At the bottom of the tree, Tom and Mark's name appeared. Tom's eyes followed the trunk of the tree up to the first tree branch. There he saw his mom and dad's name. Again, his eyes followed up to the next branch, where he saw William's name.

"Are you my great-grandfather?" asked Tom with a mix of incredulity and excitement.

"No, greater still," joked Little Eagle. "If you follow the patrilineal line, you will find your father, Ray; your grandfather, William; your great-grandfather, Josef; and then me—Little Eagle."

"How can that be? How can you go from being an American Indian to being a German immigrant? I know that Great-Grandpa Josef was brought over here by his parents ... his German parents," insisted Tom.

"For a moment, Tom," said Little Eagle, "imagine that you are a movie star. You could play the role of a football player. Later, you could play the role of a mountain climber. Still later, you could play the role of a biplane pilot. This means that you would know a little bit about being those things, but you would still be Tom Miller.

"Now, imagine your spirit being free to choose whatever life it wants to be. You could choose your nationality, your gender, your race, and your family. Better yet, you could choose what your strengths and your weaknesses would be. Much like going to the library, you can choose your own story ... your own adventure to learn life's lessons.

"Every day of your life, you can choose to read a book that opens your mind to new possibilities. Every day we choose what is real and what isn't. What it really comes down to is that the things we perceive and allow are real. Everything else is an illusion."

"So you're telling me that you are both my great-great grandfather and you are an American Indian," said Tom flatly, as though still trying to understand.

"Tom, if I pour one glass of water into ten different glasses of various shapes and color, does the liquid change into something else, or is it still water?" asked Little Eagle. "Of course, it is still water. Even when I pour it into a bowl, a vase, or a pitcher, it is still water. You, me, William, your family ... we are all from the same water. At one time, I was a German farmer who took his family across the planet in hopes of finding a better way to live. Another time, I was an American Indian who became the tribe medicine man and tried to cure my tribe of smallpox. Another time, I was a captain of a cargo ship bringing tea from India to England. For what we are going to do together, Little Eagle most closely suits who I needed to be."

"Well, who have I been?" asked Tom.

"Tom, you are absolutely fearless when it comes to asking the tough questions, and I absolutely adore that about you. However, that answer is a few years off. You have chosen to learn a few lessons, as

Tom, and I do not want to corrupt that process. Let it be enough to say that every person you have been has brought you to this point. There are scores of people waiting for you to radiate the love and wisdom you have shown heretofore ... which is unfolding within you right now. Mankind's highest potential is just around the corner and you are its vanguard."

"I don't know if I can do this by myself," whispered Tom, as he started to recognize the enormity of it all.

"But Tom, you are never alone," said Little Eagle.

Suddenly, the tree glowed brighter and hundreds and hundreds of names appeared in its branches. Toward the top of the tree, there were hundreds upon thousands of names, so crowded that no one name in particular stood out. The tree itself became larger and denser until Tom was surrounded in golden leaves. Little Eagle grabbed a handful and threw them into the air. With a sense of relief and wonderment, Tom laughed until tears of joy shone on his face. When he awoke the next morning, Tom noticed a single gold-colored leaf in his shoe. He smiled.

The trip back home was a quiet one as both William and Tom reflected about the past two months and all the changes that had taken place. Each of them wondered what the ramifications of these changes would be. Tom was most concerned with more short-term changes. He had been programming for a better relationship with Mark and with school. He hoped that he would have the same success that he had with making money. Making money was a nice thing, but he was sure going to miss hanging out with Sera.

Tom came out of his reverie as they pulled up to his house. Since it was Friday, he knew that his mom and dad would be at work. Tom's heart beat faster as he saw that Mark's car was in the garage. All the conflicts that he'd had with Mark came to mind in a flash. The mockery, the ridicule, and the condescending manner of his brother's behavior over the past couple of years threatened to crash over him. But then he thought of what Little Eagle had told him. Things were different now. It quickly became a mantra. He repeated the words over and over in his head. A quick look over to a smiling and confident William gave Tom even more reassurance. It was enough.

Tom got out of the Jeep and went around back to get his bag. As he came around the other side, he noticed that William had not gotten out. He was still sitting in the driver's seat with a slight grin on his face.

"You're not coming in, are you?" observed Tom.

"No, I think I will leave you in the same manner that I absconded with you. It keeps up my wizardly reputation and air of mystery. Seriously, it's your time now."

Tom and William exchanged a firm handshake and a smile. They each knew that they would be speaking again soon. With his familiar grin and a nod, William turned the vehicle around and headed down the gravel road for parts unknown. Tom watched until he could no longer see him.

Chapter 23 – Homecoming

Tom hoisted his bag over his shoulder and entered the house. Like many things, it seemed both familiar and different simultaneously. He saw the standard disorder that the kitchen should be in on a workday for his parents. Hastily eaten meals and half cups of beverages still sat on the table. Seeing that it needed to be straightened up, he did it. He thought for sure that his brother would hear him in the kitchen and come in and startle him, but he didn't. Tom finished making the kitchen look presentable and then made his way up to his bedroom. From inside the room, he heard the bedsprings creak. Mark was in his room! If Mark had caught him in his room, he would have punched him in the arm several times really hard.

Tom pushed his door open to see Mark lying on his bed, eating potato chips, and playing his video games. At first, Tom was very angry. Just as he was getting ready to yell at Mark, Tom remembered the look he got from William before he left. Instead, Tom entered the room as though William was directly behind him. In his head, he repeated his mantra.

"Hey!" said Mark with surprise, "what are you doing home?"

"I thought I should get back into the swing of things before school starts. Have we traded rooms while I was away?" asked Tom.

"No, this is still your room," said Mark.

"OK, I'm going to make myself something to eat and then come back and take a nap. Please have your mess cleaned up by then."

He dropped his bag on the floor and left the room while Mark sat on the bed with his mouth hanging open—empty of any retort or insult. Tom had redefined their relationship without a punch or harsh word. The changes at home had begun.

Tom sat at the table eating a peanut butter and jelly sandwich while flipping through the magazines that his parents subscribed to regularly. While doing so, he came across a newsletter from the bank that his mom worked at and noticed that they were looking to replace the person responsible for information technology. He immediately got on the phone and called Felipe. While he was dialing, Mark came downstairs and looked back and forth, from Tom to the kitchen sink, in amazement that he had cleaned up the place.

"Hola. Felipe?"

"Sí, quién habla?"

"It's Tom. How are you?"

"Cómo está? How am I? I am fine. Muy bien. Where are you?"

"I'm home. I called because I just came across a possible job for you that is about two to three hours away. It's at the bank where my mom works. They're looking for an information technology person. Is this something you can do?" asked Tom.

"Probably, but I would have to speak to the manager there to know what their expectations are," said Felipe.

"Well, the manager happens to be my mom. I'll have her call you after dinner, if that's cool with you?" asked Tom.

"Sounds great. I will wait for a call between eight o'clock and nine o'clock. Is that OK?" asked Felipe.

"Sure. If not, I'll let you know."

Tom said goodbye and turned to see Mark staring at him as though he were from another planet.

"What the hell did Grandpa feed you while you were gone," asked Mark.

"He fed me all kinds of cool stuff. Why?" replied Tom.

"You look really different," said Mark.

Tom grabbed the other half of his sandwich and started toward the stairs. He stopped suddenly and looked at his brother. Apparently, he had not been doing too much around the house. Mark was not as tan as Tom, and their physiques were now nearly identical. Tom was still shorter than Mark, but now it was only by a margin of less than two inches. Hard work, good food, and decent living had done more for Tom than Mark realized.

"Guess you think you're hot stuff now?" said Mark with his hand outstretched to shake Tom's hand.

As Tom shook his brother's hand, he had a sudden flash that Mark was going to slap him with his other hand. Immediately, Tom embraced his brother with a strong bear hug, just like the ones he used while trying to move trees. Not only did he give his brother a good squeeze, he picked him up off of the floor! Mark was shocked, surprised, and bewildered all at the same time. Tom didn't even drop his sandwich.

"I missed you too, bro," said Tom as he released his brother.

Mark stood frozen and just stared at his brother. Tom gave him a smile, bounded up the stairs, and disappeared into his room. Grabbing his bag, he flopped down on his bed and smiled. He gave a mental thank you to both his grandpa and to Little Eagle for preparing him for this unique homecoming. He opened his bag, and wedged in among his clothes were two books on Tesla. Grandpa must have slipped them there when he wasn't looking. Someday, when he understood the science and diagrams involved, he wanted to build a Tesla coil. He knew his grandpa would be the one to conspire with on such a project. After he put his things away, he opened one of the books and read until he fell asleep. Sometime afterward, he and Little Eagle had a good time congratulating each other.

Tom was awakened by the smell of chicken frying. He had not had fried chicken in more than two months, and he was ready for it. He came downstairs and saw his mom at the refrigerator and his dad at the kitchen table, paying a couple of bills. Hearing the footsteps, Karen turned around.

"Tom! Oh my goodness! Tom, you've grown like a weed!" squealed Karen as she quickly enveloped Tom in a hug.

"Oh Mom," said Tom as he tried to downplay his mother's enthusiasm. Actually, he enjoyed it, even though he would never admit it.

"Son, you have really bulked up over the past several weeks. What did Grandpa feed you?" asked Ray.

226

"Mark asked the same thing when he saw me. I knew I was getting muscles because the sleeves on my shirts started to feel tight," said Tom with a widening smile.

After a quick hug from his dad, Tom sat down and told them of his experiences at Grandpa's house. He told them about the experiments in the barn, the research, Sid and Quan, the trees, the uncommon topics of discussion, driving the Jeep, the storm, being rescued by Felipe, meeting the Lopez family, and his friend Sera.

All of this discussion took place before, during, and after dinner, so that when Tom finished with his stories it was already getting late in the evening. He told them of finishing the tree project and painting Felipe's house while clearing the table from dinner. Suddenly, he remembered the conversation with Felipe and told his mom about his need for a job. She wrote down his phone number and said she'd look into it on Monday, when she went back to work.

"That's really going to mean a lot because he's the only one who works in the family. Sera is home-schooled by her mom. If you could call him tonight, just to say you'll look into it on Monday, I know the whole family will feel better. Right now he has no opportunities," said Tom.

"Tom, I don't want to get his hopes up," said Karen.

"Mom, right now he has nothing to hope for ... people need something to hope for, don't they?" asked Tom.

"I guess you're right. I'll talk to him this evening," said Karen with a look of surprise. She was pleased with her son's insight.

Once the kitchen was cleaned, he followed his parents to the family room and sat down to watch TV with them. It was the first time in over two months that he had seen TV. As dumb luck would have it, they were going to watch a show that Tom had already seen. He sat with them and stared at the TV, but his thoughts were about the things he had learned with his grandpa. Suddenly, it occurred to him that Mark hadn't been there for dinner.

"So, where did Mark go?" asked Tom.

"He wanted to spend the night with some friends, and we thought it would be nice to spend an evening with just you since you had been gone so long," answered Karen.

Knowing Mark, Tom knew why he wasn't there. When he wasn't the center of attention, Mark would rather be somewhere where he could be. Knowing his parents, Tom was sure there was tension because they would have wanted the whole family together on Tom's first night home.

"He probably needed to visit his friends to make him feel better. When I came home, I gave him a hug and tossed him around a bit. Either he didn't like that or he didn't like the fact his little brother isn't so little anymore," said Tom.

Ray and Karen exchanged glances to indicate that they agreed with Tom's assessment.

"That's OK, he'll come to deal with it in his own time," said Tom.

"You sure learned how to be more intuitive while you were visiting Grandpa," said Ray.

"That, and then some," said Tom with his own version of a lopsided smile. The irony was not lost on Ray. He had seen that familiar lopsided grin for many years. Seeing the tradition continue made Ray happy.

The rest of the evening was spent enjoying each other's company. Ray and Tom spoke in more detail about the changes to William's house since Ray had last been there and Karen slipped out briefly to call Felipe. With any hope, there would be an opportunity for him at the bank.

Chapter 24 – Coincidence

During the few weeks between his homecoming and his return to school, Tom wanted to keep building on his newfound strength. For exercise, he split firewood for the coming winter and lined their driveway with yellow and purple mums. They were his mom's favorite. Quietly, Ray watched it all and was amazed at the positive transformation in his son. Mark was amazed too, but said nothing. In fact, he avoided Tom as much as possible. College classes and a part-time job made that pretty easy. The truth was that Mark did not know how to react to this new person Tom had become.

Tom also threw himself into all this activity as a way to forget the loneliness he felt being away from his grandpa and his friends. Tom had spoken to William only twice since he had been back. It was always good to hear his voice, but it wasn't the same as being in his presence. Tom also missed Sera ... more than he cared to admit. She had shared in his transformation and that made her important to him.

The question Tom wrestled with, though, was the "L" question. Did he miss her because she was a part of his changing process? Did he miss her because she was the only person his age who he saw this summer? Or did his sense of loss mean that he loved her? After several days of debating it, he decided to let go of the question of love for now.

Occasionally, Little Eagle would visit him while he slept. Tom was full of questions about the future. School, Sera, Mark, William, and Life were all topics of discussion for them. What was most vexing for Tom was the fact Little Eagle would not give him any answers. Little Eagle would just tell him that things would be fine and that he should have patience. Universal laws follow a pattern, but they do not move according to a time frame of our convenience. Little Eagle's way of putting it was this: Try not to push the river.

One dream, in particular, that Tom remembered was a lesson. He remembered sitting in a forest clearing with a circle of rocks in front of him. A small fire was whispering and popping while the flames changed colors from yellow, to blue and then to green. At his side was Little Eagle, who was watching the clouds roll by overhead. Tom had been lamenting about how he was lonely. He worried that when he went back to school, the kids would still make fun of him. After he laid his worries out, they sat in silence for a while. Little Eagle finally interrupted the silence.

"A grandfather was teaching his grandchildren about the essence of mankind. He told them that inside of each person there are two wolves. The first wolf is kind, friendly, trusting, loyal, and strong— always with a loving heart. The second wolf is apathetic, hateful, deceitful, dishonorable, and weak. These two wolves, which live inside each person, are constantly at war with each other; both of them fighting for dominance and control of how we behave.

"After a few moments of silence one of the grandchildren asked which wolf will win the battle.

The grandfather replied, 'The one you feed.'"

When the light of comprehension dawned in Tom's eyes, Little Eagle smiled and said, "Remember, things are different now."

It was this dream that kept Tom from reverting back to his former self whenever Mark gave him an occasional unkind look or word. This only happened a few times before Mark, finally, just stopped talking to him. The roles that each of them had played before Tom left had changed. Tom was no longer playing the role of the little brother/victim, and Mark was at a loss. Eventually, he would have to realize he, too, would need to discover a new role. Maybe this would be one of the things he would learn in college.

Another change that took place was that Tom lost contact with Felipe. He had tried to call him a few days before school started and only got the electronic message that the phone had been disconnected. Why would Felipe have his phone disconnected unless things had really become financially desperate? Tom went to his mental movie theater and imagined Felipe, Elena, and Serafina living in a nice house with plenty of everything. He imagined them being happy with where they were and what they were doing. When he wasn't imagining that, he was hoping any setback was only temporary.

Tom's first day of school was similar to his first day back home. All of his friends and acquaintances commented on how different he looked. Others, who did not know him so well, said nothing to him, but unabashedly stared at him. To distract himself from all of the attention, he kept remembering the things he learned from his grandpa and Little Eagle. Suddenly, Tom's reverie was broken as he noticed an attractive girl with dark hair that reminded him of black satin. She had a stack of books balanced on her knee and propped up against a locker. With her other hand, she was trying to open her locker and hold onto her class schedule at the same time. With a rush of excitement he hurried behind her and, with a grin of mischievousness, he said loudly, "Serafina!"

She jumped and her books went flying. She whipped around, ready to smack someone for scaring her. She had her arm bent back, as if to throw a baseball, when it stopped in midair. Her emotions swayed the opposite direction as she recognized her prankster friend.

"Tom!" she squealed as she wrapped her arms around him and started jumping up and down.

Without any sense of embarrassment, he gave her a hug back and started jumping up and down with her. People looked on with amazement and curiosity as Tom made a scene with this new girl. They would certainly be the subject of discussion at lunch. They both started talking at the same time. They laughed again.

"I was hoping that I would meet you and tell you all of the things that have been going on. In just the past week, both Mom and Dad got jobs and we moved into a house not far from here. We don't have a phone yet, so I couldn't call you," said Sera.

"Why didn't you use your dad's cell phone?" asked Tom.

"Dad got rid of it about two weeks ago because it was too expensive," replied Sera, "but now that's not a problem!"

"Did your dad get the job at the bank?" asked Tom.

"Yes, he did. In fact, he got it last week!" said Sera.

"Why didn't my mom tell me?" wondered Tom.

"Because it was supposed to be a surprise," replied Sera with a widening smile.

"This stuff is absolutely amazing!" exclaimed Tom, "I was in my movie theater hoping ... no, programming, that something like this would happen. Man, this stuff is amazing!"

"I'll tell you what's amazing," said Sera as she lowered her voice, "I have been dreaming of an American Indian boy named Little Eagle. He told me that we would find a place to live, that I would be meeting you today and what's around the corner for all of us ... you, me, and William!"

Tom stood frozen. Her words rang through his brain.

"You ... you ... know Little Eagle?" stammered Tom.

"Tom, I have been dreaming about him every night this week. He has told me a bunch of stuff. I have to tell you, but I can't go into it right now," said Sera.

Tom looked around as though everything had gone into slow motion. He noticed that some people continued to stare at him. Others had gone back to what they were doing before the commotion. As the school bell rang through the halls, he came back to reality and bent down to help Sera pick up her books. He held on to them as Sera opened her locker, sorted through the books she needed, and replaced the rest.

"Tom, we need to look at those books William gave you. In there is a Tesla device we need to build as soon as possible. If you imagine a stack of dominoes ready to fall, the device will serve as the first one," said Sera.

"This is all ... amazing. If this didn't happen to me I'd never believe it. How in the world can all this be happening all at once? People are treating me different. Mark isn't picking on me anymore. I was really lonely and then you show up here. Little Eagle appears to you and me? Now, I am supposed to build some Tesla device with you and William. What does it all mean?"

"It means," said Sera, "that things are different now. The future is ours to shape."

Suggested Readings

- *A Way of Being* by Carl Rogers
- *The Celestine Prophecy* by James Redfield
- *Edgar Cayce: The Sleeping Prophet* by Jess Stearn
- *Entangled Minds: Extrasensory Experiences in a Quantum Reality* by Dean I. Radin
- *Essential Reiki: A Complete Guide to an Ancient Healing Art* by Diane Stein
- *Hands of Light: A Guide to Healing Through the Human Energy Field* by Barbara Brennan
- *Illusions: The Adventures of a Reluctant Messiah* by Richard Bach
- *The Intention Experiment: Using Your Thoughts to Change Your Life* by Lynne McTaggart
- *Journeys Out of the Body* by Robert Monroe
- *The Only Dance There Is* by Ram Dass
- *Reiki: A Comprehensive Guide* by Pamela Miles
- *Reiki: The Healing Touch* by William Lee Rand
- *The Silva Mind Control Method* by Jose Silva
- *Toward A Psychology of Being* by Abraham Maslow
- *Wizard: The Life and Times of Nikola Tesla: Biography of a Genius* by Marc J. Seifer

About the Author

John is a child of the 1970s and grew up around Indianapolis, Indiana. In his youth, he delivered newspapers, detasseled corn, went cow tipping, and studied music. He is an award-winning bass/baritone soloist who was the youngest member of the Indianapolis Opera Theater, opened for the Oak Ridge Boys, and performed for President Reagan all before his twentieth birthday. He double majored at Marian College in both English and Music and continued to sing in local theaters and churches and write for the college newspaper.

Life events pre-empted his desired Masters Degree in ancient medieval literature and led to an interest in pharmaceutical research, which he pursued for more than a decade. During this same period, he returned to school to become a registered nurse. Always curious, he physically traveled to Western Europe, the Caribbean, Canada, and almost all of the United States. His sense of curiosity included mental adventures in astral projection, remote viewing, Usui reiki, and Silva Mind Method. Through his various practices, his enthusiasm in metaphysics is continually renewed.

After publishing several shorter works of poetry and prose, this is his first novel. John is single and is a licensed nurse and National Certified Guardian. He lives in Sarasota, Florida, where cows are scarce but margarita glasses are abundant. Questions or comments for the author can be directed to alchemists.heir@gmail.com.

Made in the USA
Charleston, SC
18 February 2012